# THE
# SOUL'S
# AWAKENING

*This work is dedicated to the many teachers and authors who have shared their wisdom and insight into the compelling and liberating symbology offered in our everyday world.*

*It is offered as a stepping stone to all who would join them on this path to self-knowledge, spiritual freedom and fulfillment.*

*Robert*

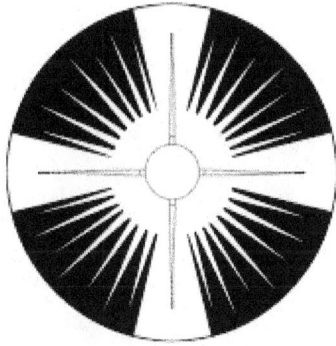

# THE
# SOUL'S
# AWAKENING

## Using Symbology and Spiritual Numerology

*"Truth For Insightful Transformation"*

Robert M. Waldon, ND, PhD

Reunion Press
17664 Greenridge Road
Hidden Valley Lake, CA95467
(800) 919-2392

ISBN: 0-9706315-3-7

First Printing, 1987
Second Printing, 2003
Third Printing, 2014

# INDEX

# ABOUT THIS WORK

Over the years I have become familiar with many different self-help, personal growth and spiritual development programs ranging from the traditional to the esoteric to the "New Age". My personal interest has always been to discover the underlying similarities in all of these approaches, with the belief that the highest truth will become more clearly known and understood by seeing where we all are joined, where we are One. It is at the level where we recognize our Oneness and Wholeness that I find my greatest peace.

So it is for me with Symbology and Spiritual Numerology. There is a very basic level at which all of the apparently divergent or differing systems, programs and interpretations are in agreement. This represents a high level of truth from which all of the various systems have evolved to serve the specific needs and desires of the groups or individuals involved in their formulation.

What I have attempted to present here is a personal workbook designed to share with you what I consider to be the highest and best from all of the various systems I have come in contact with. It is designed to be as free from "interpretation" as possible to allow you the greatest possible freedom to discover your own highest truth. From your own personal experiences and deep inner knowing you will bring to this work precisely the meaning which will have the greatest significance to you as you travel along your path.

A note about the **PERSONAL INDEX**: The personal index is a personal worksheet and represents your "road map" on the initial journey through this workbook. You will fill it in based on your work in the first chapter on Calculations. It is much easier to spend the relatively short amount of time necessary to do all of your calculations ahead of time so that you may then proceed, uninterrupted by "detail", through the balance of the workbook.

For easy future reference, there is a space on your Personal Index to record the page number which specifically relates to each aspect of your inquiry. Additional Personal Index sheets have been provided at the end of the workbook so that you may copy them and use them for family and friends as you share your discoveries.

Welcome to your **SOUL'S AWAKENING**.

Robert Waldon, ND, PhD

# SYMBOLS AS KEYS TO YOUR SELF

Robert Waldon, ND, PhD

## SYMBOLS  AS  KEYS  TO YOURSELF

There is but one learning with many possible lessons made available to us. All we need to do is **totally** "get" one, and we have gotten it all. The learning is to unconditionally love your Self. As you approach that unconditionality, your sense of Self expands to eventually include all and everyone. In this, you achieve the essence of your God-ness, your true Goodness.

Whenever you don't love someone, it is because you don't know them well enough. It is always a call to invest more of yourself in getting to know them better, not to stay away from them. The same is true in your relationship with your Self.

This book could be seen as a collection of facts and information. Information is not the truth. **Love is the truth**. Information is designed to "bump into" any areas of resistance, any barriers to full remembrance and knowing of your Self, and to break you free to recognize that all is a lie, except Love.

This book is not to tell you about you. It is not to be "learned". It is to be **used** by you as a tool, to the extent that it continues to have value for you. It is not an end, but a beginning. It is a "bare bones" outline, a skeleton for you to flesh out and use as a learning tool based on the meaning you give to it. You fill in the outline with your own inner knowingness, experiences and interpretations based on what's up for you now and what will lead you to your next expansion.

## SYMBOLOGY AND SPIRITUAL NUMEROLOGY

The world around us is a world of our creation and represents a reflection of our selves. We project aspects of our being onto the "screen" of life and then learn from the "movie" we are seeing/living.

All that we will ever need to know is to be found within ourselves—the answers to all our questions, the insights into why we are the way we are, information about why we are here, what we are to do, how we are to interact with others. In short, the truth of our Self is to be found within our Self.

Many people have blocked, to a greater or lesser degree, their own access to that inner knowledge. Until they restore the true sense of their wholeness and reawaken to fully knowing themselves directly, the second best source of self-knowing is to be found in symbols. This book is about a symbolic system directly linked to you and your life choices at a basic or core level.

The purpose in using Symbology and Spiritual Numerology is to assist you in re-awakening to the Truth about yourself, to remind you of who and what you, yourSelf, already are and why you are here at this time. Through the use of this tool, you can get reacquainted with aspects of your own character, your inherent skills and abilities, strengths and weaknesses, your life purpose and your heart's desire. You can also gain insight into life's challenges which you have chosen as opportunities for personal growth.

Symbology and Spiritual Numerology can also assist you in your relationships with others. You can locate areas of past Soul connections and current Soul connections as well as current worldly and spiritual challenges. These insights can help you transform all of your relationships into mutually supportive, unconditionally loving relationships, which is the underlying purpose for our being together.

Our lives, as we live them now, are only a selective remembering of parts of the truth. As we allow in other parts, the total picture becomes more obvious, like linking more pieces in a jig saw puzzle or uncovering more letters in "hangman". We wake up by injecting more truth into our lives, experiencing greater and fuller truths than our limited selves would normally allow.

The true learner surrenders to the teaching of life. Teachers, be they books or individuals, are only "carriers" with momentary value. It is important to stay open to each next step and not get stuck or stopped anywhere. Respond to the moment. Be in "natural" relationship with the world. Be in the world and with the flow of the world, but not part of fixation or form.

Surrender is the gentle release of all opinions, reasons or need to understand, and opens you to the great peace which comes from trusting in the way of Spirit, in the way of Nature. Heavy processing is only called forth when there is internal resistance. Once you have accepted that which you have called for to set you free, there is only joy in being with it. Deny nothing. Make way for everything.

## JUDGMENT AND FORGIVENESS

As you look at numbers and symbols, it is important to do so without judgment or comparison. No "part" in this drama of life is more important or better than any other. All parts are necessary to the whole. In fact, we each have all parts within us. The current focus apparent in our lives is the experience our Soul is calling for now to balance our perfect expression.

To judge your creation is to distort it and leave it stuck. To Love it is to be able to appreciate it and change it. That is true freedom. You create your experience of your past in each present moment. This is evidenced every time you have an upset with a friend and later "make up". The original event or conflict has not changed, but you have joined with your friend in seeing it (therefore experiencing it) differently. You have "made up" a new past.

It is one thing to "erase" the past, but true forgiveness is experienced when you can see the entire past and see all of the goodness, beauty and whole-ness (holiness). Look at the blocks to doing or being all that you are. Then forgive and let yourself fully be and fully receive from every moment.

Lack of forgiveness is the primary factor which keeps us stuck in old, outmoded and unwanted behavior and thought patterns and keeps others stuck in old, unwanted roles they are playing for our benefit. Forgiveness set us all free.

Forgiveness is seeing the Love in all your choices and the choices of others.

Forgiveness is the process of erasing all that is not whole and good and beautiful.

Forgiveness is noticing and releasing all blocks to perfect love.

Forgiveness is recognizing judgment as an error in perception.

Forgiveness is seeing only good in all that is.

Forgiveness is knowing there is love in everything.

Forgiveness is choosing a free, happy life and giving the full expression of that life to others.

Forgiveness is knowing I am a gift to all as they are a gift to me. Life is for giving and we are the gift.

Forgiveness is knowing there is value in all that is and, therefore, receiving the value and the learning with gratitude.

Forgiveness is seeing what we look for.
>           I forgive myself for:      limiting myself
>                                       rejecting myself
>                                       denying myself
>                                       judging myself

It is also helpful to do each forgiveness in two parts.
I forgive _____ for _____ and I forgive myself for _____ .

Examples:
"I forgive others for their ignorance and lack of love and I forgive my-self for believing I was unlovable."
"I forgive you mother for leaving me and I forgive myself for withhold-ing my love from you."

## AFFIRMATIONS

Seeing the best is seeing the Truth.

Do not focus on what is not working. Just recognize where you are "off purpose" by the lack of joy experienced. Then focus on more joy.

Every thought creates a result. Negative or fearful thinking creates a negative life experience. Positive or happy thinking creates a good life and happy outlook. Some of both may create a neutral or conflicted effect on our life experiences. Negative experiences can be changed as a result of consistent positive thinking.

**Affirmations** are statements of truth that are consciously taken into one's mind by repetitively writing, speaking and listening to them. The purpose of affirmations is to erase from the mind all negative thought forms or beliefs that we have falsely learned. Thoughts of limitation, lack and littleness are released and replaced with thoughts of freedom, abundance and magnificence.

A simple description of the way in which we create our life experiences as a product of our thinking:

> Our life energy is expressed through our conscious and unconscious beliefs creating a life experience of our own creation. When we think we deserve pain, we look for it, choose it and set up painful relationships and experiences simply to prove ourselves right.

To heal or change a negative life experience, the following steps are suggested:

1. Forgive yourself and others for mistakenly choosing negativity and feeding yourself negative thoughts.
2. Erase, release and cancel all negative beliefs and thoughts.
3. Consciously choose to plant seeds of positive thoughts in your mind and pay attention to these ideas until they grow into happy life experiences.

The process is like gardening and you are the gardener. The garden is your life experience. Take note of what you have grown in the garden of your life. If it has not nourished you, acknowledge this and choose to change what you grow. Release all judgment of previous choices. Pull out the "weeds" and non-nourishing thoughts. Plant what you believe to be the most healthy opportunities for your entire being.

Some useful suggestions for doing affirmations:

1. Write, speak and listen to your affirmation 1 to 20 times a day. Each time you write the affirmation, write the "mind chatter" and/or the emotional response which comes up within you. This is the old, "negative" programming in your subconscious coming up to be embraced and cleared. By writing it down each time, whatever it is your mind is saying to you, you bring it out in the open and allow it to be released. Do this process until it clears, until there is no more mind chatter and you are emotionally neutral. (Note: Do not be fooled by a state of apathy or despair in which you may become "numb" to what is being said inside. Continuing through this point back into aliveness will bring new feelings and thoughts to be cleared until you are at peace.)

2. The optimum times for gardening your mind are upon awakening and just before going to bed.

3. Tape record your affirmations and listen to them as you fall off to sleep or travel in your car.

4. Use no more than 3 affirmations at a time.

5. Usually 1 to 2 weeks of daily affirmation will clear the block.

6. Write affirming poems or songs to sing to yourself throughout the day.

Some helpful general affirmations are:

1. My mind automatically erases all negative thoughts.
   I now choose to have only happy thinking.
2. It is fun, safe and easy for me to let go of what I no longer need.
   I now choose to experience what is truly best for me.
3. I now have a clear, quiet, happy mind.
4. I now quickly recognize and release all blocks to love, happiness and inner peace.
5. I am open and willing.
6. Everything always works more exquisitely than I can plan.
7. I love myself, therefore I choose the best in life.

There are affirmations throughout the book to assist you in developing your Self and coming to know the truth about various aspects of who you are. Use these and go on from there to create your own, for this work and for every aspect of you life.

## RECEIVING INNER GUIDANCE

Soul's Awakening is a process of consulting your Higher Self, of finding that you have all the answers within you.

Inner Listening is the conscious willingness to open to the inner authority, the Voice of God, Holy Spirit, the Higher Self within each of us. All beings have the capacity to tune into Divine guidance naturally.

As we let go of worldly thoughts and experience trust and love for God, we can focus on the place of peace in our heart, and open ourselves to channel the highest Good.

By asking for the help and knowledge we need, we immediately receive the Divine answer.

By following what we hear in faith, we learn to trust Divine Will always leads to health, happiness and perfect Peace in all our affairs.

Guidelines:
1. Use a notebook or journal or tape recorder to record all that transpires in your dialogue with Spirit.
2. Give a prayer or blessing to begin, either aloud or written.
3. Set aside the parental or judging mind. Set aside adult facts, logic and need to understand.
4. Become peaceful and go inside to the innocent, trusting child.
5. Be as a child, willing to ask questions, listen and freely express all that concerns you.
6. Be open and willing. "I am open and willing to receive what is good for me now."
7. Ask for what you want and be willing to receive it.
8. As you tune in more finely to the Inner Voice, all questions are answered, all problems solved, all fears and guilts are healed instantly and all direction and purpose is given to our lives.
9. Listen and follow one day at a time and you shall know God and live in Peace.

You will know your Higher Voice as the voice that brings peace, openness, the end of conflict and creates clarity. Any fear-filled or fear producing thoughts are of the ego. From daily practice of inner listening, we soon learn to trust our Selves and follow the Inner Authority in ALL we do. Our lives work more perfectly than we can plan.

Robert Waldon, ND, PhD

## OUR SYMBOLIC TOOLS

Ideally, the entire world is your symbolic tool. You give everything in this world all the meaning it has for you. **Believing is seeing**. What you expect, you look for. What you look for, you see in all events and relationships.

You need to consciously agree to see yourself (and willingly, eagerly learn about yourself) in the meaning you project onto the events and people around you, the "symbols" of your Self in the world. If you are willing to see the meaning you give your symbols, you are willing and able to better know your Self.

In this book, you will focus on those symbols most closely and most obviously related to you. These symbols are derived from your most basic choices of name and birth date in this lifetime. As your journey to Soul's Awakening progresses, you will learn to see and love your Self in the creation of life as it unfolds around you. By loving all aspects of the whole **in you**, you come to know and love your wholeness. You then become willing to see the wholeness in everyone, no matter what aspect they are playing, and you move into a state of unconditional love for Self and others.

Know that there are no numbers or symbols which are any better then, higher than, holier, more exalted, more desirable, more powerful, or any one of the "comparatively greater than's" than any other number or symbol. We all have within us all attributes of all numbers and symbols. Each of us is completely whole and holy. In truth, we are One, and therefore, equally good (equally of God).

Using the analogy of a jigsaw puzzle, we have taken the "picture" of our wholeness and cut it into little pieces and scattered those pieces on our own personal tabletop. We are each in the process of putting that puzzle back together so that we can once again see and recognize our wholeness and therefore be able to see the wholeness of everyone else. Some people do puzzles by starting with all the edge pieces. Some start by working on specific colors. Each of us has his own method so none of us will be working on the same "piece" as anyone else. Who is to judge the relative merit of any particular piece currently being handled by any of us? It may, in fact, be our last piece, or one of the last few. The same is true for each of us. So avoid the temptation of the world to indulge in comparisons. When we judge, it is merely an indication that we are somehow "off purpose" in some area of our own life and we are calling to be awakened to getting back on purpose.

This workbook is designed to increase your level of awareness so that you can stay more surely on purpose and, in doing so, guide others to their own perfection by your example.

# CALCULATIONS

Robert Waldon, ND, PhD

# CALCULATIONS

**IMPORTANT:**
All calculations for each area described in this workbook will be covered here. For your easy reference, a **PERSONAL INDEX** is included so that you can **do all your calculations at one time,** enter them on your Personal Index and then **use the Personal Index for all your future work**.

### Basic Information
All information is based on the two primary symbols associated with your presence here at this time as described in the previous chapter. You will be using your **birth date** and your full **birth name**, regardless of any name changes you may have made since that time.

NOTE: Name changes will **add** a dimension or create a more focused emphasis on certain areas and you may want to do calculations for any and all name changes which you have chosen to see any shifts which may have been triggered. However, the basic energy that you bring and that related directly to the essence of your being is still contained in the name you chose at birth.

### Addition
In most cases, numbers are reduced to single digit numbers by adding each digit in your number to the others and continuing to do that until a one digit sum is achieved. For example, for the year 1945:
$1 + 9 + 4 + 5 = 19$
$1 + 9 = 10$
$1 + 0 = 1$

### Master Numbers
Master Numbers are the primary exception to this rule. Master numbers are the double digit numbers with repeated digits, i.e. 11, 22, 33, 44, 55, 66, 77, 88 and 99. These numbers have special significance in many areas of symbology and you will be told when and where to look for them.

Master Numbers represent unique and highly developed spiritual gifts that you bring with you for the manifestation of change and the expression of Spirit on earth in this lifetime. The presence of Master Numbers indicates a responsibility you have chosen to carry out in service to mankind. Manifestation of the full potential of your gift depends on your attunement with your Higher/Spiritual Self and your selfless motivation and dedication in determining how best to express your gift in the highest service of All.

ALTERNATE FORMS OF ADDITION will be sometimes used to "discover" otherwise hidden Master Numbers for certain areas of your work. These will be described in the appropriate areas.

12

# PERSONAL INDEX

(You will fill this chart in from the Chapter on Calculations.)

| LINE | | Number/ Symbol | Personal Page | Book # |
|------|---|---|---|---|
| 1 | Lifetime Symbol | _____ | _____ | ----43 |
| 2 | Spiritual Symbol | _____ | _____ | ----43 |
| 3 | Personal Cycle | _____ | _____ | ----59 |
| 4 | Universal Year | _____ | _____ | ----73 |
| 5 | Personal Year | _____ | _____ | ----73 |
| | | | | |
| 6 | Outer Harmony | _____ | _____ | ----82 |
| 7 | Inner Peace | _____ | _____ | ----84 |
| 8 | Past Accomplishments | _____ | _____ | ----86 |
| 9 | Spiritual Path | _____ | _____ | ----98 |
| 10 | God's Gift | _____ | _____ | ----90 |
| | | | | |
| 11 | Physical | _____ | _____ | ---101 |
| 12 | Emotional | _____ | _____ | ---103 |
| 13 | Mental | _____ | _____ | ---105 |
| 14 | Spiritual Creativity | _____ | _____ | ---108 |
| | | | | |
| 15 | Collective Experience | _____ | _____ | ---116 |
| 16 | Life Path | _____ | _____ | ---116 |
| 17 | Ultimate Lifetime Goal | _____ | _____ | ---116 |
| 18 | Balance on Life Path | _____ | _____ | ---123 |
| 19 | Soul's Urge | _____ | _____ | ---126 |
| 20 | How You Are Seen | _____ | _____ | ---130 |
| 21 | Growth | _____ | _____ | ---134 |
| | | | | |
| 22 | Balancing Expression | _____ | _____ | ---139 |

## BIRTH MONTH

Numbers to enter on Personal Index
Find your birth month in the left hand column.
Read across to find what number to enter
on the specified lines in your PERSONAL INDEX.

| MONTH | ENTER LINE 6 | ENTER LINE 11 |
|---|---|---|
| JANUARY | 1 | 1 |
| FEBRUARY | 2 | 2 |
| MARCH | 3 | 3 |
| APRIL | 4 | 4 |
| MAY | 5 | 5 |
| JUNE | 6 | 6 |
| JULY | 7 | 7 |
| AUGUST | 8 | 8 |
| SEPTEMBER | 9 | 9 |
| OCTOBER | 10 | 1 |
| NOVEMBER | 11 | 11 |
| DECEMBER | 3 | 3 |

## BIRTH DAY

Numbers to enter on Personal Index
Find your birth day in the left hand column.
Read across to find what number to enter
on the specified lines in your PERSONAL INDEX.

| DAY | ENTER LINE 7 | ENTER LINE 12 |
|-----|--------------|---------------|
| 1 | 1 | 1 |
| 2 | 2 | 2 |
| 3 | 3 | 3 |
| 4 | 4 | 4 |
| 5 | 5 | 5 |
| 6 | 6 | 6 |
| 7 | 7 | 7 |
| 8 | 8 | 8 |
| 9 | 9 | 9 |
| 10 | 10 | 1 |
| 11 | 11 | 11 |
| 12 | 3 | 3 |
| 13 | 4 | 4 |
| 14 | 5 | 5 |
| 15 | 6 | 6 |
| 16 | 7 | 7 |
| 17 | 8 | 8 |
| 18 | 9 | 9 |
| 19 | 10 | 1 |
| 20 | 2 | 2 |
| 21 | 3 | 3 |
| 22 | 4 | 22 |
| 23 | 5 | 5 |
| 24 | 6 | 6 |
| 25 | 7 | 7 |
| 26 | 8 | 8 |
| 27 | 9 | 9 |
| 28 | 10 | 1 |
| 29 | 11 | 11 |
| 30 | 3 | 3 |
| 31 | 4 | 4 |

## BIRTH YEAR

Numbers to enter on Personal Index
Find your birth year in the left hand column.
Read across to find what number to enter
on the specified lines in your PERSONAL INDEX.

| YEAR | Enter Line 8 | Enter Line 10 | Enter Line 13 |
|------|------|------|------|
| 1921 | 4 | 3 | 22 |
| 1922 | 5 | 4 | 5 |
| 1923 | 6 | 5 | 6 |
| 1924 | 7 | 6 | 7 |
| 1925 | 8 | 7 | 8 |
| 1926 | 9 | 8 | 9 |
| 1927 | 10 | 9 | 1 |
| 1928 | 11 | 10 | 11 |
| 1929 | 3 | 11 | 3 |
| 1930 | 4 | 3 | 22 |
| 1931 | 5 | 4 | 5 |
| 1932 | 6 | 5 | 33 |
| 1933 | 7 | 6 | 7 |
| 1934 | 8 | 7 | 8 |
| 1935 | 9 | 8 | 9 |
| 1936 | 10 | 9 | 1 |
| 1937 | 11 | 10 | 11 |
| 1938 | 3 | 11 | 3 |
| 1939 | 4 | 3 | 22 |
| 1940 | 5 | 4 | 5 |
| 1941 | 6 | 5 | 6 |
| 1942 | 7 | 6 | 7 |
| 1943 | 8 | 7 | 8 |
| 1944 | 9 | 8 | 9 |
| 1945 | 10 | 9 | 1 |
| 1946 | 11 | 10 | 11 |
| 1947 | 3 | 11 | 3 |
| 1948 | 4 | 3 | 22 |
| 1949 | 5 | 4 | 5 |
| 1950 | 6 | 5 | 6 |
| 1951 | 7 | 6 | 7 |
| 1952 | 8 | 7 | 8 |
| 1953 | 9 | 8 | 9 |
| 1954 | 10 | 9 | 1 |
| 1955 | 11 | 10 | 11 |

# BIRTH YEAR

Numbers to enter on Personal Index
Find your birth year in the left hand column.
Read across to find what number to enter
on the specified lines in your PERSONAL INDEX.

| YEAR | Enter Line 8 | Enter Line 10 | Enter Line 13 |
|------|------|------|------|
| 1956 | 3 | 11 | 3 |
| 1957 | 4 | 3 | 22 |
| 1958 | 5 | 4 | 5 |
| 1959 | 6 | 5 | 33 |
| 1960 | 7 | 6 | 7 |
| 1961 | 8 | 7 | 8 |
| 1962 | 9 | 8 | 9 |
| 1963 | 10 | 9 | 1 |
| 1964 | 11 | 10 | 11 |
| 1965 | 3 | 11 | 3 |
| 1966 | 4 | 3 | 22 |
| 1967 | 5 | 4 | 5 |
| 1968 | 6 | 5 | 33 |
| 1969 | 7 | 6 | 7 |
| 1970 | 8 | 7 | 8 |
| 1971 | 9 | 8 | 9 |
| 1972 | 10 | 9 | 1 |
| 1973 | 11 | 10 | 11 |
| 1974 | 3 | 11 | 3 |
| 1975 | 4 | 3 | 22 |
| 1976 | 5 | 4 | 5 |
| 1977 | 6 | 5 | 33 |
| 1978 | 7 | 6 | 7 |
| 1979 | 8 | 7 | 8 |
| 1980 | 9 | 8 | 9 |
| 1981 | 10 | 9 | 1 |
| 1982 | 11 | 10 | 11 |
| 1983 | 3 | 11 | 3 |
| 1984 | 4 | 3 | 22 |
| 1985 | 5 | 4 | 5 |
| 1986 | 6 | 5 | 33 |
| 1987 | 7 | 6 | 7 |
| 1988 | 8 | 7 | 8 |
| 1989 | 9 | 8 | 9 |
| 1990 | 10 | 9 | 1 |

Robert Waldon, ND, PhD

## BIRTH YEAR

Numbers to enter on Personal Index
Find your birth year in the left hand column.
Read across to find what number to enter
on the specified lines in your PERSONAL INDEX.

| YEAR | Enter Line 8 | Enter Line 10 | Enter Line 13 |
|------|------|------|------|
| 1991 | 11 | 10 | 11 |
| 1992 | 3 | 11 | 3 |
| 1993 | 4 | 3 | 22 |
| 1994 | 5 | 4 | 5 |
| 1995 | 6 | 5 | 33 |
| 1996 | 7 | 6 | 7 |
| 1997 | 8 | 7 | 8 |
| 1998 | 9 | 8 | 9 |
| 1999 | 10 | 9 | 1 |
| 2000 | 2 | 10 | 11 |
| 2001 | 3 | 1 | 3 |
| 2002 | 4 | 2 | 22 |
| 2003 | 5 | 3 | 5 |
| 2004 | 6 | 4 | 6 |
| 2005 | 7 | 5 | 7 |
| 2006 | 8 | 6 | 8 |
| 2007 | 9 | 7 | 9 |
| 2008 | 10 | 8 | 1 |
| 2009 | 11 | 9 | 11 |
| 2010 | 3 | 10 | 3 |
| 2011 | 4 | 11 | 4 |
| 2012 | 5 | 3 | 5 |
| 2013 | 6 | 4 | 33 |
| 2014 | 7 | 5 | 7 |
| 2015 | 8 | 6 | 8 |
| 2016 | 9 | 7 | 9 |
| 2017 | 10 | 8 | 10 |
| 2018 | 11 | 9 | 11 |
| 2019 | 3 | 10 | 3 |
| 2020 | 4 | 2 | 22 |
| 2021 | 5 | 3 | 5 |
| 2022 | 6 | 4 | 6 |
| 2023 | 7 | 5 | 7 |
| 2024 | 8 | 6 | 8 |
| 2025 | 9 | 7 | 9 |

## TOTAL BIRTH DATE CALCULATION

In calculating your Total Birth Date, you will add the month plus the day plus the year of your birth.

          Example:

          June 15, 1952

$$
\begin{array}{r}
6 \\
15 \\
+\ \underline{1952} \\
1973
\end{array}
$$

You will then look up this total on the following charts and enter the appropriate number as indicated.

## TOTAL BIRTHDATE

Find your total month + day + year of birth in the left hand column. Read across to find what number to enter on the specified lines in your PERSONAL INDEX.

| TOTAL | Enter Line 1 | Enter Line 2 | Enter Line 9 | Enter Line 14 | Enter Line 16 | Enter Line 18 |
|---|---|---|---|---|---|---|
| 1900 | 10 | 1 | 10 | 1 | 55 | 1 |
| 1901 | 11 | 2 | 11 | 2 | 11 | 2 |
| 1902 | 12 | 3 | 3 | 3 | 3 | 3 |
| 1903 | 13 | 4 | 4 | 22 | 22 | 4 |
| 1904 | 14 | 5 | 5 | 5 | 5 | 5 |
| 1905 | 15 | 6 | 6 | 6 | 6 | 6 |
| 1906 | 16 | 7 | 7 | 7 | 7 | 7 |
| 1907 | 17 | 8 | 8 | 8 | 8 | 8 |
| 1908 | 18 | 9 | 9 | 9 | 9 | 9 |
| 1909 | 19/10/1 | 19/10/1 | 10 | 1 | 1 | 1 |
| 1910 | 11 | 2 | 11 | 11 | 11 | 2 |
| 1911 | 12 | 3 | 3 | 3 | 3 | 3 |
| 1912 | 13 | 4 | 4 | 22 | 22 | 4 |
| 1913 | 14 | 5 | 5 | 5 | 5 | 5 |
| 1914 | 15 | 6 | 6 | 33 | 33 | 6 |
| 1915 | 16 | 7 | 7 | 7 | 7 | 7 |
| 1916 | 17 | 8 | 8 | 8 | 8 | 8 |
| 1917 | 18 | 9 | 9 | 9 | 9 | 9 |
| 1918 | 19/10/1 | 19/10/1 | 10 | 1 | 1 | 1 |
| 1919 | 20 | 2 | 11 | 11 | 11 | 2 |
| 1920 | 12 | 3 | 3 | 3 | 3 | 3 |
| 1921 | 13 | 4 | 4 | 22 | 22 | 4 |
| 1922 | 14 | 5 | 5 | 5 | 5 | 5 |
| 1923 | 15 | 6 | 6 | 6 | 6 | 6 |
| 1924 | 16 | 7 | 7 | 7 | 7 | 7 |
| 1925 | 17 | 8 | 8 | 8 | 44 | 8 |
| 1926 | 18 | 9 | 9 | 9 | 9 | 9 |
| 1927 | 19/10/1 | 19/10/1 | 10 | 1 | 1 | 1 |
| 1928 | 20 | 2 | 11 | 11 | 11 | 2 |
| 1929 | 21 | 3 | 3 | 3 | 3 | 3 |
| 1930 | 13 | 4 | 4 | 22 | 22 | 4 |
| 1931 | 14 | 5 | 5 | 5 | 5 | 5 |
| 1932 | 15 | 6 | 6 | 33 | 33 | 6 |
| 1933 | 16 | 7 | 7 | 7 | 7 | 7 |
| 1934 | 17 | 8 | 8 | 8 | 44 | 8 |
| 1935 | 18 | 9 | 9 | 9 | 45 | 9 |
| 1936 | 19/10/1 | 19/10/1 | 10 | 1 | 55 | 1 |
| 1937 | 20 | 2 | 11 | 11 | 11 | 2 |
| 1938 | 21 | 3 | 3 | 3 | 3 | 3 |
| 1939 | 22/0 | 4 | 4 | 22 | 22 | 4 |
| 1940 | 14 | 5 | 5 | 5 | 5 | 5 |

## TOTAL BIRTHDATE

Find your total month + day + year of birth in the left hand column. Read across to find what number to enter on the specified lines in your PERSONAL INDEX.

| TOTAL | Enter Line 1 | Enter Line 2 | Enter Line 9 | Enter Line 14 | Enter Line 16 | Enter Line 18 |
|---|---|---|---|---|---|---|
| 1941 | 15 | 6 | 6 | 6 | 6 | 6 |
| 1942 | 16 | 7 | 7 | 7 | 7 | 7 |
| 1943 | 17 | 8 | 8 | 8 | 44 | 8 |
| 1944 | 18 | 9 | 9 | 9 | 9 | 9 |
| 1945 | 19/10/1 | 19/10/1 | 10 | 1 | 55 | 1 |
| 1946 | 20/11 | 2 | 11 | 11 | 11 | 2 |
| 1947 | 21/12 | 3 | 3 | 3 | 66 | 3 |
| 1948 | 22/0 | 4 | 4 | 22 | 22 | 4 |
| 1949 | 14 | 5 | 5 | 5 | 5 | 5 |
| 1950 | 15 | 6 | 6 | 6 | 6 | 6 |
| 1951 | 16 | 7 | 7 | 7 | 7 | 7 |
| 1952 | 17 | 8 | 8 | 8 | 8 | 8 |
| 1953 | 18 | 9 | 9 | 9 | 9 | 9 |
| 1954 | 19/10/1 | 19/10/1 | 10 | 1 | 55 | 1 |
| 1955 | 20/11 | 2 | 11 | 11 | 11 | 2 |
| 1956 | 21/12 | 3 | 3 | 3 | 66 | 3 |
| 1957 | 22/0 | 4 | 4 | 22 | 22 | 4 |
| 1958 | 14 | 5 | 5 | 5 | 77 | 5 |
| 1959 | 15 | 6 | 6 | 33 | 33 | 6 |
| 1960 | 16 | 7 | 7 | 7 | 7 | 7 |
| 1961 | 17 | 8 | 8 | 8 | 8 | 8 |
| 1962 | 18 | 9 | 9 | 9 | 9 | 9 |
| 1963 | 19/10/1 | 19/10/1 | 10 | 1 | 1 | 1 |
| 1964 | 20/11 | 2 | 11 | 11 | 11 | 2 |
| 1965 | 21/12 | 3 | 3 | 3 | 66 | 3 |
| 1966 | 22/0 | 4 | 4 | 22 | 22 | 4 |
| 1967 | 14 | 5 | 5 | 5 | 77 | 5 |
| 1968 | 15 | 6 | 6 | 33 | 33 | 6 |
| 1969 | 16 | 7 | 7 | 7 | 88 | 7 |
| 1970 | 17 | 8 | 8 | 8 | 8 | 8 |
| 1971 | 18 | 9 | 9 | 9 | 9 | 9 |
| 1972 | 19/10/1 | 19/10/1 | 10 | 1 | 1 | 1 |
| 1973 | 20/11 | 2 | 11 | 11 | 11 | 2 |
| 1974 | 21/12 | 3 | 3 | 3 | 3 | 3 |
| 1975 | 22/0 | 4 | 4 | 22 | 22 | 4 |
| 1976 | 14 | 5 | 5 | 5 | 77 | 5 |
| 1977 | 15 | 6 | 6 | 33 | 33 | 6 |
| 1978 | 16 | 7 | 7 | 7 | 88 | 7 |
| 1979 | 17 | 8 | 8 | 8 | 8 | 8 |
| 1980 | 18 | 9 | 9 | 9 | 99 | 9 |

## TOTAL BIRTHDATE

Find your total month + day + year of birth in the left hand column. Read across to find what number to enter on the specified lines in your PERSONAL INDEX.

| TOTAL | Enter Line 1 | Enter Line 2 | Enter Line 9 | Enter Line 14 | Enter Line 16 | Enter Line 18 |
|---|---|---|---|---|---|---|
| 1981 | 19/10/1 | 19/10/1 | 10 | 1 | 1 | 1 |
| 1982 | 20/11 | 2 | 11 | 11 | 11 | 2 |
| 1983 | 21/12 | 3 | 3 | 3 | 3 | 3 |
| 1984 | 22/0 | 4 | 4 | 22 | 22 | 4 |
| 1985 | 14 | 5 | 5 | 5 | 5 | 5 |
| 1986 | 15 | 6 | 6 | 33 | 33 | 6 |
| 1987 | 16 | 7 | 7 | 7 | 88 | 7 |
| 1988 | 17 | 8 | 8 | 8 | 8 | 8 |
| 1989 | 18 | 9 | 9 | 9 | 99 | 9 |
| 1990 | 19/10/1 | 19/10/1 | 10 | 1 | 1 | 1 |
| 1991 | 20/11 | 2 | 11 | 11 | 11 | 2 |
| 1992 | 21/12 | 3 | 3 | 3 | 3 | 3 |
| 1993 | 22/0 | 4 | 4 | 22 | 22 | 4 |
| 1994 | 14 | 5 | 5 | 5 | 5 | 5 |
| 1995 | 15 | 6 | 6 | 33 | 33 | 6 |
| 1996 | 16 | 7 | 7 | 7 | 7 | 7 |
| 1997 | 17 | 8 | 8 | 8 | 8 | 8 |
| 1998 | 18 | 9 | 9 | 9 | 99 | 9 |
| 1999 | 19/10/1 | 19/10/1 | 10 | 1 | 1 | 1 |
| 2000 | 20/11 | 2 | 2 | 2 | 2 | 2 |
| 2001 | 21/12 | 3 | 3 | 3 | 3 | 3 |
| 2002 | 22 | 4 | 4 | 4 | 22 | 4 |
| 2003 | 14 | 5 | 5 | 5 | 5 | 5 |
| 2004 | 15 | 6 | 6 | 6 | 6 | 6 |
| 2005 | 16 | 7 | 7 | 7 | 7 | 7 |
| 2006 | 17 | 8 | 8 | 8 | 8 | 8 |
| 2007 | 18 | 9 | 9 | 9 | 9 | 9 |
| 2008 | 19/10/1 | 19/10/1 | 10 | 1 | 1 | 1 |
| 2009 | 11 | 2 | 11 | 11 | 11 | 2 |
| 2010 | 21/12 | 3 | 3 | 3 | 3 | 3 |
| 2011 | 22/0 | 4 | 4 | 4 | 22 | 4 |
| 2012 | 14 | 5 | 5 | 5 | 5 | 5 |
| 2013 | 15 | 6 | 6 | 6 | 33 | 6 |
| 2014 | 16 | 7 | 7 | 7 | 7 | 7 |
| 2015 | 17 | 8 | 8 | 8 | 8 | 8 |
| 2016 | 18 | 9 | 9 | 9 | 9 | 9 |
| 2017 | 19/10/1 | 19/10/1 | 10 | 1 | 1 | 1 |
| 2018 | 11 | 2 | 11 | 11 | 11 | 2 |
| 2019 | 21/12 | 3 | 3 | 3 | 3 | 3 |
| 2020 | 22/0 | 4 | 4 | 4 | 22 | 4 |

## TOTAL BIRTHDATE

Find your total month + day + year of birth in the left hand column. Read across to find what number to enter on the specified lines in your PERSONAL INDEX.

| TOTAL | Enter Line 1 | Enter Line 2 | Enter Line 9 | Enter Line 14 | Enter Line 16 | Enter Line 18 |
|---|---|---|---|---|---|---|
| 2021 | 14 | 5 | 5 | 5 | 5 | 5 |
| 2022 | 15 | 6 | 6 | 6 | 6 | 6 |
| 2023 | 16 | 7 | 7 | 7 | 7 | 7 |
| 2024 | 17 | 8 | 8 | 8 | 44 | 8 |
| 2025 | 18 | 9 | 9 | 9 | 9 | 9 |
| 2026 | 19/10/1 | 19/10/1 | 10 | 1 | 1 | 1 |
| 2027 | 11 | 2 | 11 | 11 | 11 | 2 |
| 2028 | 21/12 | 3 | 3 | 3 | 3 | 3 |
| 2029 | 22/0 | 4 | 4 | 4 | 4 | 4 |
| 2030 | 14 | 5 | 5 | 5 | 5 | 5 |
| 2031 | 15 | 6 | 6 | 6 | 33 | 6 |
| 2032 | 16 | 7 | 7 | 7 | 7 | 7 |
| 2033 | 17 | 8 | 8 | 8 | 8 | 8 |
| 2034 | 18 | 9 | 9 | 9 | 9 | 9 |
| 2035 | 19/10/1 | 19/10/1 | 10 | 1 | 55 | 1 |
| 2036 | 11 | 2 | 11 | 11 | 11 | 2 |
| 2037 | 21/12 | 3 | 3 | 3 | 3 | 3 |
| 2038 | 22/0 | 4 | 4 | 4 | 22 | 4 |
| 2039 | 14 | 5 | 5 | 5 | 5 | 5 |
| 2040 | 15 | 6 | 6 | 6 | 6 | 6 |
| 2041 | 16 | 7 | 7 | 7 | 7 | 7 |
| 2042 | 17 | 8 | 8 | 8 | 44 | 8 |
| 2043 | 18 | 9 | 9 | 9 | 9 | 9 |
| 2044 | 19/10/1 | 19/10/1 | 10 | 1 | 1 | 1 |
| 2045 | 11 | 2 | 11 | 11 | 11 | 2 |
| 2046 | 21/12 | 3 | 3 | 3 | 66 | 3 |
| 2047 | 22/0 | 4 | 4 | 4 | 22 | 4 |
| 2048 | 14 | 5 | 5 | 5 | 5 | 5 |
| 2049 | 15 | 6 | 6 | 6 | 33 | 6 |
| 2050 | 16 | 7 | 7 | 7 | 7 | 7 |
| 2051 | 17 | 8 | 8 | 8 | 44 | 8 |
| 2052 | 18 | 9 | 9 | 9 | 9 | 9 |
| 2053 | 19/10/1 | 19/10/1 | 10 | 1 | 55 | 1 |
| 2054 | 11 | 2 | 11 | 11 | 11 | 2 |
| 2055 | 21/12 | 3 | 3 | 3 | 66 | 3 |
| 2056 | 22/0 | 4 | 4 | 4 | 22 | 4 |
| 2057 | 14 | 5 | 5 | 5 | 77 | 5 |
| 2058 | 15 | 6 | 6 | 6 | 33 | 6 |
| 2059 | 16 | 7 | 7 | 7 | 7 | 7 |
| 2060 | 17 | 8 | 8 | 8 | 8 | 8 |

Robert Waldon, ND, PhD

## CYCLES

To determine what Cycle of your life you are currently in, find your **birth month** on the following pages then read across from your **birth day** to see what calendar year you enter each of your lifetime Cycles. (Note: Not all Cycles are listed here, only those which would apply to this portion of your life.)

You enter each Cycle on your birthday of the calendar year indicated and continue in that Cycle until your birthday in the calendar year that begins your next Cycle. The Cycle that you are currently in is the last one that **begins on or before your birthday** in this calendar year.

Enter on **Line 3** of your Personal Index the cycle you are currently in.

# JANUARY
(enter path name on line 3 of your Personal Index)

|    | Builder | Heart | Leadership | Success | Love | Freedom | Harmony |
|----|---------|-------|------------|---------|------|---------|---------|
| 1  | 1998 | 2008 | 2018 | 2028 | 2038 | 2048 | 2058 |
| 2  | 1997 | 2007 | 2017 | 2027 | 2037 | 2047 | 2057 |
| 3  | 1996 | 2006 | 2016 | 2026 | 2036 | 2046 | 2056 |
| 4  | 1995 | 2005 | 2015 | 2025 | 2035 | 2045 | 2055 |
| 5  | 1994 | 2004 | 2014 | 2024 | 2034 | 2044 | 2054 |
| 6  | 1993 | 2003 | 2013 | 2023 | 2033 | 2043 | 2053 |
| 7  | 1992 | 2002 | 2012 | 2022 | 2032 | 2042 | 2052 |
| 8  | 1991 | 2001 | 2011 | 2021 | 2031 | 2041 | 2051 |
| 9  | 1990 | 2000 | 2010 | 2020 | 2030 | 2040 | 2050 |
| 10 | 1989 | 1999 | 2009 | 2019 | 2029 | 2039 | 2049 |
| 11 | 1988 | 1998 | 2008 | 2018 | 2028 | 2038 | 2048 |
| 12 | 1987 | 1997 | 2007 | 2017 | 2027 | 2037 | 2047 |
| 13 | 1986 | 1996 | 2006 | 2016 | 2026 | 2036 | 2046 |
| 14 | 1985 | 1995 | 2005 | 2015 | 2025 | 2035 | 2045 |
| 15 | 1984 | 1994 | 2004 | 2014 | 2024 | 2034 | 2044 |
| 16 | 1983 | 1993 | 2003 | 2013 | 2023 | 2033 | 2043 |
| 17 | 1982 | 1992 | 2002 | 2012 | 2022 | 2032 | 2042 |
| 18 | 1981 | 1991 | 2001 | 2011 | 2021 | 2031 | 2041 |
| 19 | 1980 | 1990 | 2000 | 2010 | 2020 | 2030 | 2040 |
| 20 | 1979 | 1989 | 1999 | 2009 | 2019 | 2029 | 2039 |
| 21 | 1978 | 1988 | 1998 | 2008 | 2018 | 2028 | 2038 |
| 22 | 1977 | 1987 | 1997 | 2007 | 2017 | 2027 | 2037 |
| 23 | 1976 | 1986 | 1996 | 2006 | 2016 | 2026 | 2036 |
| 24 | 1975 | 1985 | 1995 | 2005 | 2015 | 2025 | 2035 |
| 25 | 1974 | 1984 | 1994 | 2004 | 2014 | 2024 | 2034 |
| 26 | 1973 | 1983 | 1993 | 2003 | 2013 | 2023 | 2033 |
| 27 | 1972 | 1982 | 1992 | 2002 | 2012 | 2022 | 2032 |
| 28 | 1971 | 1981 | 1991 | 2001 | 2011 | 2021 | 2031 |
| 29 | 1970 | 1980 | 1990 | 2000 | 2010 | 2020 | 2030 |
| 30 | 1969 | 1979 | 1989 | 1999 | 2009 | 2019 | 2029 |
| 31 | 1968 | 1978 | 1988 | 1998 | 2008 | 2018 | 2028 |

Robert Waldon, ND, PhD

## FEBRUARY
(enter path name on line 3 of your Personal Index)

|    | Builder | Heart | Leadership | Success | Love | Freedom | Harmony |
|----|---------|-------|------------|---------|------|---------|---------|
| 1  | 1997 | 2007 | 2017 | 2027 | 2037 | 2047 | 2057 |
| 2  | 1996 | 2006 | 2016 | 2026 | 2036 | 2046 | 2056 |
| 3  | 1995 | 2005 | 2015 | 2025 | 2035 | 2045 | 2055 |
| 4  | 1994 | 2004 | 2014 | 2024 | 2034 | 2044 | 2054 |
| 5  | 1993 | 2003 | 2013 | 2023 | 2033 | 2043 | 2053 |
| 6  | 1992 | 2002 | 2012 | 2022 | 2032 | 2042 | 2052 |
| 7  | 1991 | 2001 | 2011 | 2021 | 2031 | 2041 | 2051 |
| 8  | 1990 | 2000 | 2010 | 2020 | 2030 | 2040 | 2050 |
| 9  | 1989 | 1999 | 2009 | 2019 | 2029 | 2039 | 2049 |
| 10 | 1988 | 1998 | 2008 | 2018 | 2028 | 2038 | 2048 |
| 11 | 1987 | 1997 | 2007 | 2017 | 2027 | 2037 | 2047 |
| 12 | 1986 | 1996 | 2006 | 2016 | 2026 | 2036 | 2046 |
| 13 | 1985 | 1995 | 2005 | 2015 | 2025 | 2035 | 2045 |
| 14 | 1984 | 1994 | 2004 | 2014 | 2024 | 2034 | 2044 |
| 15 | 1983 | 1993 | 2003 | 2013 | 2023 | 2033 | 2043 |
| 16 | 1982 | 1992 | 2002 | 2012 | 2022 | 2032 | 2042 |
| 17 | 1981 | 1991 | 2001 | 2011 | 2021 | 2031 | 2041 |
| 18 | 1980 | 1990 | 2000 | 2010 | 2020 | 2030 | 2040 |
| 19 | 1979 | 1989 | 1999 | 2009 | 2019 | 2029 | 2039 |
| 20 | 1978 | 1988 | 1998 | 2008 | 2018 | 2028 | 2038 |
| 21 | 1977 | 1987 | 1997 | 2007 | 2017 | 2027 | 2037 |
| 22 | 1976 | 1986 | 1996 | 2006 | 2016 | 2026 | 2036 |
| 23 | 1975 | 1985 | 1995 | 2005 | 2015 | 2025 | 2035 |
| 24 | 1974 | 1984 | 1994 | 2004 | 2014 | 2024 | 2034 |
| 25 | 1973 | 1983 | 1993 | 2003 | 2013 | 2023 | 2033 |
| 26 | 1972 | 1982 | 1992 | 2002 | 2012 | 2022 | 2032 |
| 27 | 1971 | 1981 | 1991 | 2001 | 2011 | 2021 | 2031 |
| 28 | 1970 | 1980 | 1990 | 2000 | 2010 | 2020 | 2030 |
| 29 | 1969 | 1979 | 1989 | 1999 | 2009 | 2019 | 2029 |

# MARCH
(enter path name on line 3 of your Personal Index)

| | Builder | Heart | Leadership | Success | Love | Freedom | Harmony |
|---|---|---|---|---|---|---|---|
| 1 | 1996 | 2006 | 2016 | 2026 | 2036 | 2046 | 2056 |
| 2 | 1995 | 2005 | 2015 | 2025 | 2035 | 2045 | 2055 |
| 3 | 1994 | 2004 | 2014 | 2024 | 2034 | 2044 | 2054 |
| 4 | 1993 | 2003 | 2013 | 2023 | 2033 | 2043 | 2053 |
| 5 | 1992 | 2002 | 2012 | 2022 | 2032 | 2042 | 2052 |
| 6 | 1991 | 2001 | 2011 | 2021 | 2031 | 2041 | 2051 |
| 7 | 1990 | 2000 | 2010 | 2020 | 2030 | 2040 | 2050 |
| 8 | 1989 | 1999 | 2009 | 2019 | 2029 | 2039 | 2049 |
| 9 | 1988 | 1998 | 2008 | 2018 | 2028 | 2038 | 2048 |
| 10 | 1987 | 1997 | 2007 | 2017 | 2027 | 2037 | 2047 |
| 11 | 1986 | 1996 | 2006 | 2016 | 2026 | 2036 | 2046 |
| 12 | 1985 | 1995 | 2005 | 2015 | 2025 | 2035 | 2045 |
| 13 | 1984 | 1994 | 2004 | 2014 | 2024 | 2034 | 2044 |
| 14 | 1983 | 1993 | 2003 | 2013 | 2023 | 2033 | 2043 |
| 15 | 1982 | 1992 | 2002 | 2012 | 2022 | 2032 | 2042 |
| 16 | 1981 | 1991 | 2001 | 2011 | 2021 | 2031 | 2041 |
| 17 | 1980 | 1990 | 2000 | 2010 | 2020 | 2030 | 2040 |
| 18 | 1979 | 1989 | 1999 | 2009 | 2019 | 2029 | 2039 |
| 19 | 1978 | 1988 | 1998 | 2008 | 2018 | 2028 | 2038 |
| 20 | 1977 | 1987 | 1997 | 2007 | 2017 | 2027 | 2037 |
| 21 | 1976 | 1986 | 1996 | 2006 | 2016 | 2026 | 2036 |
| 22 | 1975 | 1985 | 1995 | 2005 | 2015 | 2025 | 2035 |
| 23 | 1974 | 1984 | 1994 | 2004 | 2014 | 2024 | 2034 |
| 24 | 1973 | 1983 | 1993 | 2003 | 2013 | 2023 | 2033 |
| 25 | 1972 | 1982 | 1992 | 2002 | 2012 | 2022 | 2032 |
| 26 | 1971 | 1981 | 1991 | 2001 | 2011 | 2021 | 2031 |
| 27 | 1970 | 1980 | 1990 | 2000 | 2010 | 2020 | 2030 |
| 28 | 1969 | 1979 | 1989 | 1999 | 2009 | 2019 | 2029 |
| 29 | 1968 | 1978 | 1988 | 1998 | 2008 | 2018 | 2028 |
| 30 | 1967 | 1977 | 1987 | 1997 | 2007 | 2017 | 2027 |
| 31 | 1966 | 1976 | 1986 | 1996 | 2006 | 2016 | 2026 |

Robert Waldon, ND, PhD

## APRIL
(enter path name on line 3 of your Personal Index)

| | Builder | Heart | Leadership | Success | Love | Freedom | Harmony |
|---|---|---|---|---|---|---|---|
| 1 | 1995 | 2005 | 2015 | 2025 | 2035 | 2045 | 2055 |
| 2 | 1994 | 2004 | 2014 | 2024 | 2034 | 2044 | 2054 |
| 3 | 1993 | 2003 | 2013 | 2023 | 2033 | 2043 | 2053 |
| 4 | 1992 | 2002 | 2012 | 2022 | 2032 | 2042 | 2052 |
| 5 | 1991 | 2001 | 2011 | 2021 | 2031 | 2041 | 2051 |
| 6 | 1990 | 2000 | 2010 | 2020 | 2030 | 2040 | 2050 |
| 7 | 1989 | 1999 | 2009 | 2019 | 2029 | 2039 | 2049 |
| 8 | 1988 | 1998 | 2008 | 2018 | 2028 | 2038 | 2048 |
| 9 | 1987 | 1997 | 2007 | 2017 | 2027 | 2037 | 2047 |
| 10 | 1986 | 1996 | 2006 | 2016 | 2026 | 2036 | 2046 |
| 11 | 1985 | 1995 | 2005 | 2015 | 2025 | 2035 | 2045 |
| 12 | 1984 | 1994 | 2004 | 2014 | 2024 | 2034 | 2044 |
| 13 | 1983 | 1993 | 2003 | 2013 | 2023 | 2033 | 2043 |
| 14 | 1982 | 1992 | 2002 | 2012 | 2022 | 2032 | 2042 |
| 15 | 1981 | 1991 | 2001 | 2011 | 2021 | 2031 | 2041 |
| 16 | 1980 | 1990 | 2000 | 2010 | 2020 | 2030 | 2040 |
| 17 | 1979 | 1989 | 1999 | 2009 | 2019 | 2029 | 2039 |
| 18 | 1978 | 1988 | 1998 | 2008 | 2018 | 2028 | 2038 |
| 19 | 1977 | 1987 | 1997 | 2007 | 2017 | 2027 | 2037 |
| 20 | 1976 | 1986 | 1996 | 2006 | 2016 | 2026 | 2036 |
| 21 | 1975 | 1985 | 1995 | 2005 | 2015 | 2025 | 2035 |
| 22 | 1974 | 1984 | 1994 | 2004 | 2014 | 2024 | 2034 |
| 23 | 1973 | 1983 | 1993 | 2003 | 2013 | 2023 | 2033 |
| 24 | 1972 | 1982 | 1992 | 2002 | 2012 | 2022 | 2032 |
| 25 | 1971 | 1981 | 1991 | 2001 | 2011 | 2021 | 2031 |
| 26 | 1970 | 1980 | 1990 | 2000 | 2010 | 2020 | 2030 |
| 27 | 1969 | 1979 | 1989 | 1999 | 2009 | 2019 | 2029 |
| 28 | 1968 | 1978 | 1988 | 1998 | 2008 | 2018 | 2028 |
| 29 | 1967 | 1977 | 1987 | 1997 | 2007 | 2017 | 2027 |
| 30 | 1966 | 1976 | 1986 | 1996 | 2006 | 2016 | 2026 |

# MAY
(enter path name on line 3 of your Personal Index)

| | Builder | Heart | Leadership | Success | Love | Freedom | Harmony |
|---|---|---|---|---|---|---|---|
| 1 | 1994 | 2004 | 2014 | 2024 | 2034 | 2044 | 2054 |
| 2 | 1993 | 2003 | 2013 | 2023 | 2033 | 2043 | 2053 |
| 3 | 1992 | 2002 | 2012 | 2022 | 2032 | 2042 | 2052 |
| 4 | 1991 | 2001 | 2011 | 2021 | 2031 | 2041 | 2051 |
| 5 | 1990 | 2000 | 2010 | 2020 | 2030 | 2040 | 2050 |
| 6 | 1989 | 1999 | 2009 | 2019 | 2029 | 2039 | 2049 |
| 7 | 1988 | 1998 | 2008 | 2018 | 2028 | 2038 | 2048 |
| 8 | 1987 | 1997 | 2007 | 2017 | 2027 | 2037 | 2047 |
| 9 | 1986 | 1996 | 2006 | 2016 | 2026 | 2036 | 2046 |
| 10 | 1985 | 1995 | 2005 | 2015 | 2025 | 2035 | 2045 |
| 11 | 1984 | 1994 | 2004 | 2014 | 2024 | 2034 | 2044 |
| 12 | 1983 | 1993 | 2003 | 2013 | 2023 | 2033 | 2043 |
| 13 | 1982 | 1992 | 2002 | 2012 | 2022 | 2032 | 2042 |
| 14 | 1981 | 1991 | 2001 | 2011 | 2021 | 2031 | 2041 |
| 15 | 1980 | 1990 | 2000 | 2010 | 2020 | 2030 | 2040 |
| 16 | 1979 | 1989 | 1999 | 2009 | 2019 | 2029 | 2039 |
| 17 | 1978 | 1988 | 1998 | 2008 | 2018 | 2028 | 2038 |
| 18 | 1977 | 1987 | 1997 | 2007 | 2017 | 2027 | 2037 |
| 19 | 1976 | 1986 | 1996 | 2006 | 2016 | 2026 | 2036 |
| 20 | 1975 | 1985 | 1995 | 2005 | 2015 | 2025 | 2035 |
| 21 | 1974 | 1984 | 1994 | 2004 | 2014 | 2024 | 2034 |
| 22 | 1973 | 1983 | 1993 | 2003 | 2013 | 2023 | 2033 |
| 23 | 1972 | 1982 | 1992 | 2002 | 2012 | 2022 | 2032 |
| 24 | 1971 | 1981 | 1991 | 2001 | 2011 | 2021 | 2031 |
| 25 | 1970 | 1980 | 1990 | 2000 | 2010 | 2020 | 2030 |
| 26 | 1969 | 1979 | 1989 | 1999 | 2009 | 2019 | 2029 |
| 27 | 1968 | 1978 | 1988 | 1998 | 2008 | 2018 | 2028 |
| 28 | 1967 | 1977 | 1987 | 1997 | 2007 | 2017 | 2027 |
| 29 | 1966 | 1976 | 1986 | 1996 | 2006 | 2016 | 2026 |
| 30 | 1965 | 1975 | 1985 | 1995 | 2005 | 2015 | 2025 |

# JUNE
(enter path name on line 3 of your Personal Index)

|    | Builder | Heart | Leadership | Success | Love | Freedom | Harmony |
|----|---------|-------|------------|---------|------|---------|---------|
| 1  | 1993 | 2003 | 2013 | 2023 | 2033 | 2043 | 2053 |
| 2  | 1992 | 2002 | 2012 | 2022 | 2032 | 2042 | 2052 |
| 3  | 1991 | 2001 | 2011 | 2021 | 2031 | 2041 | 2051 |
| 4  | 1990 | 2000 | 2010 | 2020 | 2030 | 2040 | 2050 |
| 5  | 1989 | 1999 | 2009 | 2019 | 2029 | 2039 | 2049 |
| 6  | 1988 | 1998 | 2008 | 2018 | 2028 | 2038 | 2048 |
| 7  | 1987 | 1997 | 2007 | 2017 | 2027 | 2037 | 2047 |
| 8  | 1986 | 1996 | 2006 | 2016 | 2026 | 2036 | 2046 |
| 9  | 1985 | 1995 | 2005 | 2015 | 2025 | 2035 | 2045 |
| 10 | 1984 | 1994 | 2004 | 2014 | 2024 | 2034 | 2044 |
| 11 | 1983 | 1993 | 2003 | 2013 | 2023 | 2033 | 2043 |
| 12 | 1982 | 1992 | 2002 | 2012 | 2022 | 2032 | 2042 |
| 13 | 1981 | 1991 | 2001 | 2011 | 2021 | 2031 | 2041 |
| 14 | 1980 | 1990 | 2000 | 2010 | 2020 | 2030 | 2040 |
| 15 | 1979 | 1989 | 1999 | 2009 | 2019 | 2029 | 2039 |
| 16 | 1978 | 1988 | 1998 | 2008 | 2018 | 2028 | 2038 |
| 17 | 1977 | 1987 | 1997 | 2007 | 2017 | 2027 | 2037 |
| 18 | 1976 | 1986 | 1996 | 2006 | 2016 | 2026 | 2036 |
| 19 | 1975 | 1985 | 1995 | 2005 | 2015 | 2025 | 2035 |
| 20 | 1974 | 1984 | 1994 | 2004 | 2014 | 2024 | 2034 |
| 21 | 1973 | 1983 | 1993 | 2003 | 2013 | 2023 | 2033 |
| 22 | 1972 | 1982 | 1992 | 2002 | 2012 | 2022 | 2032 |
| 23 | 1971 | 1981 | 1991 | 2001 | 2011 | 2021 | 2031 |
| 24 | 1970 | 1980 | 1990 | 2000 | 2010 | 2020 | 2030 |
| 25 | 1969 | 1979 | 1989 | 1999 | 2009 | 2019 | 2029 |
| 26 | 1968 | 1978 | 1988 | 1998 | 2008 | 2018 | 2028 |
| 27 | 1967 | 1977 | 1987 | 1997 | 2007 | 2017 | 2027 |
| 28 | 1966 | 1976 | 1986 | 1996 | 2006 | 2016 | 2026 |
| 29 | 1965 | 1975 | 1985 | 1995 | 2005 | 2015 | 2025 |
| 30 | 1964 | 1974 | 1984 | 1994 | 2004 | 2014 | 2024 |

# JULY
(enter path name on line 3 of your Personal Index)

|    | Builder | Heart | Leadership | Success | Love | Freedom | Harmony |
|----|---------|-------|------------|---------|------|---------|---------|
| 1  | 1992 | 2002 | 2012 | 2022 | 2032 | 2042 | 2052 |
| 2  | 1991 | 2001 | 2011 | 2021 | 2031 | 2041 | 2051 |
| 3  | 1990 | 2000 | 2010 | 2020 | 2030 | 2040 | 2050 |
| 4  | 1989 | 1999 | 2009 | 2019 | 2029 | 2039 | 2049 |
| 5  | 1988 | 1998 | 2008 | 2018 | 2028 | 2038 | 2048 |
| 6  | 1987 | 1997 | 2007 | 2017 | 2027 | 2037 | 2047 |
| 7  | 1986 | 1996 | 2006 | 2016 | 2026 | 2036 | 2046 |
| 8  | 1985 | 1995 | 2005 | 2015 | 2025 | 2035 | 2045 |
| 9  | 1984 | 1994 | 2004 | 2014 | 2024 | 2034 | 2044 |
| 10 | 1983 | 1993 | 2003 | 2013 | 2023 | 2033 | 2043 |
| 11 | 1982 | 1992 | 2002 | 2012 | 2022 | 2032 | 2042 |
| 12 | 1981 | 1991 | 2001 | 2011 | 2021 | 2031 | 2041 |
| 13 | 1980 | 1990 | 2000 | 2010 | 2020 | 2030 | 2040 |
| 14 | 1979 | 1989 | 1999 | 2009 | 2019 | 2029 | 2039 |
| 15 | 1978 | 1988 | 1998 | 2008 | 2018 | 2028 | 2038 |
| 16 | 1977 | 1987 | 1997 | 2007 | 2017 | 2027 | 2037 |
| 17 | 1976 | 1986 | 1996 | 2006 | 2016 | 2026 | 2036 |
| 18 | 1975 | 1985 | 1995 | 2005 | 2015 | 2025 | 2035 |
| 19 | 1974 | 1984 | 1994 | 2004 | 2014 | 2024 | 2034 |
| 20 | 1973 | 1983 | 1993 | 2003 | 2013 | 2023 | 2033 |
| 21 | 1972 | 1982 | 1992 | 2002 | 2012 | 2022 | 2032 |
| 22 | 1971 | 1981 | 1991 | 2001 | 2011 | 2021 | 2031 |
| 23 | 1970 | 1980 | 1990 | 2000 | 2010 | 2020 | 2030 |
| 24 | 1969 | 1979 | 1989 | 1999 | 2009 | 2019 | 2029 |
| 25 | 1968 | 1978 | 1988 | 1998 | 2008 | 2018 | 2028 |
| 26 | 1967 | 1977 | 1987 | 1997 | 2007 | 2017 | 2027 |
| 27 | 1966 | 1976 | 1986 | 1996 | 2006 | 2016 | 2026 |
| 28 | 1965 | 1975 | 1985 | 1995 | 2005 | 2015 | 2025 |
| 29 | 1964 | 1974 | 1984 | 1994 | 2004 | 2014 | 2024 |
| 30 | 1963 | 1973 | 1983 | 1993 | 2003 | 2013 | 2023 |
| 31 | 1962 | 1972 | 1982 | 1992 | 2002 | 2012 | 2022 |

Robert Waldon, ND, PhD

## AUGUST
(enter path name on line 3 of your Personal Index)

|    | Builder | Heart | Leadership | Success | Love | Freedom | Harmony |
|----|---------|-------|------------|---------|------|---------|---------|
| 1  | 1991 | 2001 | 2011 | 2021 | 2031 | 2041 | 2051 |
| 2  | 1990 | 2000 | 2010 | 2020 | 2030 | 2040 | 2050 |
| 3  | 1989 | 1999 | 2009 | 2019 | 2029 | 2039 | 2049 |
| 4  | 1988 | 1998 | 2008 | 2018 | 2028 | 2038 | 2048 |
| 5  | 1987 | 1997 | 2007 | 2017 | 2027 | 2037 | 2047 |
| 6  | 1986 | 1996 | 2006 | 2016 | 2026 | 2036 | 2046 |
| 7  | 1985 | 1995 | 2005 | 2015 | 2025 | 2035 | 2045 |
| 8  | 1984 | 1994 | 2004 | 2014 | 2024 | 2034 | 2044 |
| 9  | 1983 | 1993 | 2003 | 2013 | 2023 | 2033 | 2043 |
| 10 | 1982 | 1992 | 2002 | 2012 | 2022 | 2032 | 2042 |
| 11 | 1981 | 1991 | 2001 | 2011 | 2021 | 2031 | 2041 |
| 12 | 1980 | 1990 | 2000 | 2010 | 2020 | 2030 | 2040 |
| 13 | 1979 | 1989 | 1999 | 2009 | 2019 | 2029 | 2039 |
| 14 | 1978 | 1988 | 1998 | 2008 | 2018 | 2028 | 2038 |
| 15 | 1977 | 1987 | 1997 | 2007 | 2017 | 2027 | 2037 |
| 16 | 1976 | 1986 | 1996 | 2006 | 2016 | 2026 | 2036 |
| 17 | 1975 | 1985 | 1995 | 2005 | 2015 | 2025 | 2035 |
| 18 | 1974 | 1984 | 1994 | 2004 | 2014 | 2024 | 2034 |
| 19 | 1973 | 1983 | 1993 | 2003 | 2013 | 2023 | 2033 |
| 20 | 1972 | 1982 | 1992 | 2002 | 2012 | 2022 | 2032 |
| 21 | 1971 | 1981 | 1991 | 2001 | 2011 | 2021 | 2031 |
| 22 | 1970 | 1980 | 1990 | 2000 | 2010 | 2020 | 2030 |
| 23 | 1969 | 1979 | 1989 | 1999 | 2009 | 2019 | 2029 |
| 24 | 1968 | 1978 | 1988 | 1998 | 2008 | 2018 | 2028 |
| 25 | 1967 | 1977 | 1987 | 1997 | 2007 | 2017 | 2027 |
| 26 | 1966 | 1976 | 1986 | 1996 | 2006 | 2016 | 2026 |
| 27 | 1965 | 1975 | 1985 | 1995 | 2005 | 2015 | 2025 |
| 28 | 1964 | 1974 | 1984 | 1994 | 2004 | 2014 | 2024 |
| 29 | 1963 | 1973 | 1983 | 1993 | 2003 | 2013 | 2023 |
| 30 | 1962 | 1972 | 1982 | 1992 | 2002 | 2012 | 2022 |
| 31 | 1961 | 1971 | 1981 | 1991 | 2001 | 2011 | 2021 |

# SEPTEMBER
(enter path name on line 3 of your Personal Index)

|    | Builder | Heart | Leadership | Success | Love | Freedom | Harmony |
|----|---------|-------|------------|---------|------|---------|---------|
| 1  | 1990 | 2000 | 2010 | 2020 | 2030 | 2040 | 2050 |
| 2  | 1989 | 1999 | 2009 | 2019 | 2029 | 2039 | 2049 |
| 3  | 1988 | 1998 | 2008 | 2018 | 2028 | 2038 | 2028 |
| 4  | 1987 | 1997 | 2007 | 2017 | 2027 | 2037 | 2047 |
| 5  | 1986 | 1996 | 2006 | 2016 | 2026 | 2036 | 2046 |
| 6  | 1985 | 1995 | 2005 | 2015 | 2025 | 2035 | 2045 |
| 7  | 1984 | 1994 | 2004 | 2014 | 2024 | 2034 | 2044 |
| 8  | 1983 | 1993 | 2003 | 2013 | 2023 | 2033 | 2043 |
| 9  | 1982 | 1992 | 2002 | 2012 | 2022 | 2032 | 2042 |
| 10 | 1981 | 1991 | 2001 | 2011 | 2021 | 2031 | 2041 |
| 11 | 1980 | 1990 | 2000 | 2010 | 2020 | 2030 | 2040 |
| 12 | 1979 | 1989 | 1999 | 2009 | 2019 | 2029 | 2049 |
| 13 | 1978 | 1988 | 1998 | 2008 | 2018 | 2028 | 2038 |
| 14 | 1977 | 1987 | 1997 | 2007 | 2017 | 2027 | 2037 |
| 15 | 1976 | 1986 | 1996 | 2006 | 2016 | 2026 | 2036 |
| 16 | 1975 | 1985 | 1995 | 2005 | 2015 | 2025 | 2035 |
| 17 | 1974 | 1984 | 1994 | 2004 | 2014 | 2024 | 2034 |
| 18 | 1973 | 1983 | 1993 | 2003 | 2013 | 2023 | 2033 |
| 19 | 1972 | 1982 | 1992 | 2002 | 2012 | 2022 | 2032 |
| 20 | 1971 | 1981 | 1991 | 2001 | 2011 | 2021 | 2031 |
| 21 | 1970 | 1980 | 1990 | 2000 | 2010 | 2020 | 2030 |
| 22 | 1969 | 1979 | 1989 | 1999 | 2009 | 2019 | 2029 |
| 23 | 1968 | 1978 | 1988 | 1998 | 2008 | 2018 | 2028 |
| 24 | 1967 | 1977 | 1987 | 1997 | 2007 | 2017 | 2027 |
| 25 | 1966 | 1976 | 1986 | 1996 | 2006 | 2016 | 2026 |
| 26 | 1965 | 1975 | 1985 | 1995 | 2005 | 2015 | 2025 |
| 27 | 1964 | 1974 | 1984 | 1994 | 2004 | 2014 | 2024 |
| 28 | 1963 | 1973 | 1983 | 1993 | 2003 | 2013 | 2023 |
| 29 | 1962 | 1972 | 1982 | 1992 | 2002 | 2012 | 2022 |
| 30 | 1961 | 1971 | 1981 | 1991 | 2001 | 2011 | 2021 |

## OCTOBER
(enter path name on line 3 of your Personal Index)

| | Builder | Heart | Leadership | Success | Love | Freedom | Harmony |
|---|---|---|---|---|---|---|---|
| 1 | 1989 | 1999 | 2009 | 2019 | 2029 | 2039 | 2049 |
| 2 | 1988 | 1998 | 2008 | 2018 | 2028 | 2038 | 2048 |
| 3 | 1987 | 1997 | 2007 | 2017 | 2027 | 2037 | 2047 |
| 4 | 1986 | 1996 | 2006 | 2016 | 2026 | 2036 | 2046 |
| 5 | 1985 | 1995 | 2005 | 2015 | 2025 | 2035 | 2045 |
| 6 | 1984 | 1994 | 2004 | 2014 | 2024 | 2034 | 2044 |
| 7 | 1983 | 1993 | 2003 | 2013 | 2023 | 2033 | 2043 |
| 8 | 1982 | 1992 | 2002 | 2012 | 2022 | 2032 | 2042 |
| 9 | 1981 | 1991 | 2001 | 2011 | 2021 | 2031 | 2041 |
| 10 | 1980 | 1990 | 2000 | 2010 | 2020 | 2030 | 2040 |
| 11 | 1979 | 1989 | 1999 | 2009 | 2019 | 2029 | 2039 |
| 12 | 1978 | 1988 | 1998 | 2008 | 2018 | 2028 | 2038 |
| 13 | 1977 | 1987 | 1997 | 2007 | 2017 | 2027 | 2037 |
| 14 | 1976 | 1986 | 1996 | 2006 | 2016 | 2026 | 2036 |
| 15 | 1975 | 1985 | 1995 | 2005 | 2015 | 2025 | 2035 |
| 16 | 1974 | 1984 | 1994 | 2004 | 2014 | 2024 | 2034 |
| 17 | 1973 | 1983 | 1993 | 2003 | 2013 | 2023 | 2033 |
| 18 | 1972 | 1982 | 1992 | 2002 | 2012 | 2022 | 2032 |
| 19 | 1971 | 1981 | 1991 | 2001 | 2011 | 2021 | 2031 |
| 20 | 1970 | 1980 | 1990 | 2000 | 2010 | 2020 | 2030 |
| 21 | 1969 | 1979 | 1989 | 1999 | 2009 | 2019 | 2029 |
| 22 | 1968 | 1978 | 1988 | 1998 | 2008 | 2018 | 2028 |
| 23 | 1967 | 1977 | 1987 | 1997 | 2007 | 2017 | 2027 |
| 24 | 1966 | 1976 | 1986 | 1996 | 2006 | 2016 | 2026 |
| 25 | 1965 | 1975 | 1985 | 1995 | 2005 | 2015 | 2025 |
| 26 | 1964 | 1974 | 1984 | 1994 | 2004 | 2014 | 2024 |
| 27 | 1963 | 1973 | 1983 | 1993 | 2003 | 2013 | 2023 |
| 28 | 1962 | 1972 | 1982 | 1992 | 2002 | 2012 | 2022 |
| 29 | 1961 | 1971 | 1981 | 1991 | 2001 | 2011 | 2021 |
| 30 | 1960 | 1970 | 1980 | 1990 | 2000 | 2010 | 2020 |
| 31 | 1959 | 1969 | 1979 | 1989 | 1999 | 2009 | 2019 |

# NOVEMBER
(enter path name on line 3 of your Personal Index)

| | Builder | Heart | Leadership | Success | Love | Freedom | Harmony |
|---|---|---|---|---|---|---|---|
| 1 | 1988 | 1998 | 2008 | 2018 | 2028 | 2038 | 2048 |
| 2 | 1987 | 1997 | 2007 | 2017 | 2027 | 2037 | 2047 |
| 3 | 1986 | 1996 | 2006 | 2016 | 2026 | 2036 | 2046 |
| 4 | 1985 | 1995 | 2005 | 2015 | 2025 | 2035 | 2045 |
| 5 | 1984 | 1994 | 2004 | 2014 | 2024 | 2034 | 2044 |
| 6 | 1983 | 1993 | 2003 | 2013 | 2023 | 2033 | 2043 |
| 7 | 1982 | 1992 | 2002 | 2012 | 2022 | 2032 | 2042 |
| 8 | 1981 | 1991 | 2001 | 2011 | 2021 | 2031 | 2041 |
| 9 | 1980 | 1990 | 2000 | 2010 | 2020 | 2030 | 2040 |
| 10 | 1979 | 1989 | 1999 | 2009 | 2019 | 2029 | 2039 |
| 11 | 1978 | 1988 | 1998 | 2008 | 2018 | 2028 | 2038 |
| 12 | 1977 | 1987 | 1997 | 2007 | 2017 | 2027 | 2037 |
| 13 | 1976 | 1986 | 1996 | 2006 | 2016 | 2026 | 2036 |
| 14 | 1975 | 1985 | 1995 | 2005 | 2015 | 2025 | 2035 |
| 15 | 1974 | 1984 | 1994 | 2004 | 2014 | 2024 | 2034 |
| 16 | 1973 | 1983 | 1993 | 2003 | 2013 | 2023 | 2033 |
| 17 | 1972 | 1982 | 1992 | 2002 | 2012 | 2022 | 2032 |
| 18 | 1971 | 1981 | 1991 | 2001 | 2011 | 2021 | 2031 |
| 19 | 1970 | 1980 | 1990 | 2000 | 2010 | 2020 | 2030 |
| 20 | 1969 | 1979 | 1989 | 1999 | 2009 | 2019 | 2029 |
| 21 | 1968 | 1978 | 1988 | 1998 | 2008 | 2018 | 2028 |
| 22 | 1967 | 1977 | 1987 | 1997 | 2007 | 2017 | 2027 |
| 23 | 1966 | 1976 | 1986 | 1996 | 2006 | 2016 | 2026 |
| 24 | 1965 | 1975 | 1985 | 1995 | 2005 | 2015 | 2025 |
| 25 | 1964 | 1974 | 1984 | 1994 | 2004 | 2014 | 2024 |
| 26 | 1963 | 1973 | 1983 | 1993 | 2003 | 2013 | 2023 |
| 27 | 1962 | 1972 | 1982 | 1992 | 2002 | 2012 | 2022 |
| 28 | 1961 | 1971 | 1981 | 1991 | 2001 | 2011 | 2021 |
| 29 | 1960 | 1970 | 1980 | 1990 | 2000 | 2010 | 2020 |
| 30 | 1959 | 1969 | 1979 | 1989 | 1999 | 2009 | 2019 |

# DECEMBER

(enter path name on line 3 of your Personal Index)

|    | Builder | Heart | Leadership | Success | Love | Freedom | Harmony |
|----|---------|-------|------------|---------|------|---------|---------|
| 1  | 1987 | 1997 | 2007 | 2017 | 2027 | 2037 | 2047 |
| 2  | 1986 | 1996 | 2006 | 2016 | 2026 | 2036 | 2046 |
| 3  | 1985 | 1995 | 2005 | 2015 | 2025 | 2035 | 2045 |
| 4  | 1984 | 1994 | 2004 | 2014 | 2024 | 2034 | 2044 |
| 5  | 1983 | 1993 | 2003 | 2013 | 2023 | 2033 | 2043 |
| 6  | 1982 | 1992 | 2002 | 2012 | 2022 | 2032 | 2042 |
| 7  | 1981 | 1991 | 2001 | 2011 | 2021 | 2031 | 2041 |
| 8  | 1980 | 1990 | 2000 | 2010 | 2020 | 2030 | 2040 |
| 9  | 1979 | 1989 | 1999 | 2009 | 2019 | 2029 | 2039 |
| 10 | 1978 | 1988 | 1998 | 2008 | 2018 | 2028 | 2038 |
| 11 | 1977 | 1987 | 1997 | 2007 | 2017 | 2027 | 2037 |
| 12 | 1976 | 1986 | 1996 | 2006 | 2016 | 2026 | 2036 |
| 13 | 1975 | 1985 | 1995 | 2005 | 2015 | 2025 | 2035 |
| 14 | 1974 | 1984 | 1994 | 2004 | 2014 | 2024 | 2034 |
| 15 | 1973 | 1983 | 1993 | 2003 | 2013 | 2023 | 2033 |
| 16 | 1972 | 1982 | 1992 | 2002 | 2012 | 2022 | 2032 |
| 17 | 1971 | 1981 | 1991 | 2001 | 2011 | 2021 | 2031 |
| 18 | 1970 | 1980 | 1990 | 2000 | 2010 | 2020 | 2030 |
| 19 | 1969 | 1979 | 1989 | 1999 | 2009 | 2019 | 2029 |
| 20 | 1968 | 1978 | 1988 | 1998 | 2008 | 2018 | 2028 |
| 21 | 1967 | 1977 | 1987 | 1997 | 2007 | 2017 | 2027 |
| 22 | 1966 | 1976 | 1986 | 1996 | 2006 | 2016 | 2026 |
| 23 | 1965 | 1975 | 1985 | 1995 | 2005 | 2015 | 2025 |
| 24 | 1964 | 1974 | 1984 | 1994 | 2004 | 2014 | 2024 |
| 25 | 1963 | 1973 | 1983 | 1993 | 2003 | 2013 | 2023 |
| 26 | 1962 | 1972 | 1982 | 1992 | 2002 | 2012 | 2022 |
| 27 | 1961 | 1971 | 1981 | 1991 | 2001 | 2011 | 2021 |
| 28 | 1960 | 1970 | 1980 | 1990 | 2000 | 2010 | 2020 |
| 29 | 1959 | 1969 | 1979 | 1989 | 1999 | 2009 | 2019 |
| 30 | 1958 | 1968 | 1978 | 1988 | 1998 | 2008 | 2018 |
| 31 | 1957 | 1967 | 1977 | 1987 | 1997 | 2007 | 2017 |

## PERSONAL YEAR CALCULATIONS

To calculate your Personal Year, you add the month plus the day of your birth plus the **current year** (or the year you wish to consider). Your personal year runs from your birthday in the selected year until your birthday in the following year.

Example:
The Personal Year for the individual above, looking at the year 2000, would be calculated as:

June 15, 1987

$$
\begin{array}{r}
6 \\
15 \\
+\ 2000 \\
\hline
2021
\end{array}
$$

You would then look this total up on the following charts and enter the appropriate number as indicated.

## UNIVERSAL YEAR CALCULATION

The Universal Year is merely the year in question (usually the current year) and runs from January 1 of that year through December 31. Look up the year desired on the following charts and enter the number as indicated.

Robert Waldon, ND, PhD

| UNIVERSAL YEAR | Line 4 |
| PERSONAL YEAR | Line 5 |

| | | | | | |
|---|---|---|---|---|---|
| 1951 | 16 | 1986 | 6 | 2020 | 4 |
| 1952 | 17 | 1987 | 7 | 2021 | 5 |
| 1953 | 18 | 1988 | 8 | 2022 | 6 |
| 1954 | 19 | 1989 | 9 | 2023 | 7 |
| 1955 | 20 | 1990 | 19 | 2024 | 8 |
| 1956 | 21 | 1991 | 20 | 2025 | 9 |
| 1957 | 4 | 1992 | 21 | 2026 | 10 |
| 1958 | 5 | 1993 | 4 | 2027 | 11 |
| 1959 | 6 | 1994 | 5 | 2028 | 12 |
| 1960 | 16 | 1995 | 6 | 2029 | 13 |
| 1961 | 17 | 1996 | 7 | 2030 | 5 |
| 1962 | 18 | 1997 | 8 | 2031 | 6 |
| 1963 | 19 | 1998 | 9 | 2032 | 7 |
| 1964 | 20 | 1999 | 10 | 2033 | 8 |
| 1965 | 21 | 2000 | 2 | 2034 | 9 |
| 1966 | 4 | 2001 | 3 | 2035 | 10 |
| 1967 | 5 | 2002 | 4 | 2036 | 11 |
| 1968 | 6 | 2003 | 5 | 2037 | 12 |
| 1969 | 7 | 2004 | 6 | 2038 | 13 |
| 1970 | 17 | 2005 | 7 | 2039 | 14 |
| 1971 | 18 | 2006 | 8 | 2040 | 6 |
| 1972 | 19 | 2007 | 9 | 2041 | 7 |
| 1973 | 20 | 2008 | 10 | 2042 | 8 |
| 1974 | 21 | 1974 | 21 | 2043 | 9 |
| 1975 | 4 | 2009 | 11 | 2044 | 10 |
| 1976 | 5 | 2010 | 3 | 2045 | 11 |
| 1977 | 6 | 2011 | 4 | 2046 | 12 |
| 1978 | 7 | 2012 | 5 | 2047 | 13 |
| 1979 | 8 | 2013 | 6 | 2048 | 14 |
| 1980 | 18 | 2014 | 7 | 2049 | 15 |
| 1981 | 19 | 2015 | 8 | 2050 | 7 |
| 1982 | 20 | 2016 | 9 | 2051 | 8 |
| 1983 | 21 | 2017 | 10 | 2052 | 9 |
| 1984 | 4 | 2018 | 11 | 2053 | 10 |
| 1985 | 5 | 2019 | 12 | 2054 | 11 |

## FULL BIRTH NAME

Each letter in your name is represented by the numeric value of its place in the alphabet.

| 1 | 2 | 3 | 4 | 5 | 6 | 7 | 8 | 9 |
|---|---|---|---|---|---|---|---|---|
| A | B | C | D | E | F | G | H | I |

| 10 | 11 | 12 | 13 | 14 | 15 | 16 | 17 | 18 |
|----|----|----|----|----|----|----|----|----|
| J | K | L | M | N | O | P | Q | R |

| 19 | 20 | 21 | 22 | 23 | 24 | 25 | 26 |
|----|----|----|----|----|----|----|----|
| S | T | U | V | W | X | Y | Z |

These values are usually reduced to a single digit for simplicity.

| 1 | 2 | 3 | 4 | 5 | 6 | 7 | 8 | 9 |
|---|---|---|---|---|---|---|---|---|
| A | B | C | D | E | F | G | H | I |
| J | K | L | M | N | O | P | Q | R |
| S | T | U | V | W | X | Y | Z |   |

Print your full birth name on a piece of paper with some space between the letters. Since vowels (A, E, I, O, U and Y when it is used as a vowel) and consonants are considered separately for some aspects, I recommend writing the numeric value of consonants above the consonants in your name and the numeric value of vowels below each vowel in your name. Then add total vowels, consonants and letters for first, middle and last names.

EXAMPLE:

```
9    2    9    2                    C=22
R  O  B  E  R  T                    T=33
   6     5                          V=11

4    9  1  8    3  3                C=28
M  A  R  S  H  A  L  L              T=30
   1           1                    V=2

5    3  4    5                      C=17
W  A  L  D  O  N                    T=24
   1        6                       V=7
```

```
          Total   C=67
                  Total=87=15=6
          Total   V=20
```

### Robert Waldon, ND, PhD

This is an area where it can be fun to explore alternative methods of addition to discover "hidden" Master Numbers in your name.

For example:

Looking at the total for all letters in my name as above, yields a final numeric value of 6.

As an alternative, I could have reduced first and middle name totals each to single digits before adding to the last name total to uncover the Master Number 33 (6 + 3 + 24 = 33).

Looking at total vowels, I see that 11 + 2 + 7 = 20 = 2.

Alternatively, I could have added 2 + 2 + 7 = the Master Number 11.

You might also want to play with the possibility of using the 2 digit number for all letters having an original 2 digit number to see if that creates any other possibilities.

EXAMPLE:

| 18 | | 2 | | 18 | 20 | | C=58 |
|----|---|---|---|----|----|---|------|
| **R** | **O** | **B** | **E** | **R** | **T** | | T=78 |
| | 15 | | 5 | | | | V=20 |

| 13 | | 18 | 19 | 8 | | 12 | 12 | C=82 |
|----|---|----|----|---|---|----|----|------|
| **M** | **A** | **R** | **S** | **H** | **A** | **L** | **L** | T=84 |
| | 1 | | | | 1 | | | V=2 |

| 23 | | 12 | 4 | | 14 | | C=53 |
|----|---|----|---|---|----|---|------|
| **W** | **A** | **L** | **D** | **O** | **N** | | T=69 |
| | 1 | | | 15 | | | V=16 |

Looking at total consonants, 58 reduces to 13, 10 to 1 and 53 to 8 giving 13 + 1 + 8 = the Master Number 22.
Looking at total letters, 69 reduces to 15 = 6, 84 = 12 and 78 = 15 giving 6 + 12 + 15 = the Master Number 33.

You could also play with combinations of 1 and 2 digit numbers for each letter.

For example:

```
9     2    9   2                          C=22
R  O  B  E  R  T                          T=33
   6     5                                 V=11

13    18  1  8     12  12                  C=64
M  A  R  S  H  A  L  L                     T=66
   1           1                           V=2

5     12  4     5                          C=26
W  A  L  D  O  N                           T=33
   1        6                              V=7
```

This also allows me to see that the total consonants in my name could be the Master Number 22.
Total first = 22 = 4.
Total middle = 64 = 10.
Total last = 26 = 8.
        Total, 4 + 10 + 8 = 22.

Through "playing around", I have discovered these Master Numbers in my name:

| | |
|---|---|
| Total vowels | 11 |
| Total consonants | 22 |
| Total letters | 33 |
| Total first name | 33 |
| Total middle name | 66 |
| Total last name | 33 |

It's not this "convenient" for all names. I have a good name to use for an example to show the kind of discovery that can be done.

Robert Waldon, ND, PhD

As a clue to help you discover Master Numbers within the totals, the following single digit numbers may have a Master Number behind them:

| | | | |
|---|---|---|---|
| 1 | = | 55 | (5+5=10, 1+0=1) |
| 2 | = | 11 | (1+1=2) |
| 3 | = | 66 | (6+6=12, 1+2=3) |
| 4 | = | 22 | (2+2=4) |
| 5 | = | 77 | (7+7=14, 1+4=5) |
| 6 | = | 33 | (3+3=6) |
| 7 | = | 88 | (8+8=16, 1+6=7) |
| 8 | = | 44 | (4+4=8) |
| 9 | = | 99 | (9+9=18, 1+8=9) |

## ENTER

Total for letters in all names on **Line 15** of your Personal Index.

Total vowels in all names on **Line 19**.

Total consonants in all names on **Line 20**.

Total letters in first name on **Line 21**.

## FINAL ENTRIES TO PERSONAL INDEX

In **Line 17** of your personal index you should enter the single digit or the Master Number that results from the addition of results for Lines 15 + 16. You may find it valuable to go back to some of the "pre-totals" for your calculations on Lines 15 and 16 and use those in your addition for Line 17 to see if you get any different combinations or uncover a Master Number.

# SPIRITUAL AND LIFETIME SYMBOLS

## SPIRITUAL AND LIFETIME SYMBOLS

Your Spiritual Symbol represents your Soul's purpose through all your lifetimes.

You Lifetime Symbol represents what you have come into this lifetime to learn, to do, to express, to actualize, to find out about, to become.

Your Lifetime symbol is calculated as the sum of your month, day and year of birth, expressed as a number from 11 to 22 (in this case, the Master Number 22 = 0). Your Spiritual Symbol is the Lifetime Symbol reduced to a single digit. (See Calculation section for details.)

If there is only one number representing both the Spiritual and Lifetime Symbols, it means that, in this lifetime, you are specifically working on your Soul's overall purpose. This creates a greater sense of focus and direction.

If your Lifetime Symbol is 19 (The Sun), that means that the symbols 19, 10 and 1 (Sun, Wheel Of Fortune and Magician) are **all** both your Lifetime and Spiritual Symbols. This indicates an imperative need to communicate your personal creative expressions. It creates the same sense of focus and direction mentioned above (since Spiritual and Lifetime Symbols are the same) and indicates a need to work only with those people whose vision and purpose are supportive of, or in harmony with, your own. You will be intolerant of, or unable to relate to, those who do not.

For Spiritual and Lifetime Symbols, the Master Number 22 becomes 4 (The Emperor) for the Lifetime Symbol and 0 (The Fool) for the Spiritual Symbol.

Following are attributes of each symbol and affirmations related to the expression of each. Since these symbols are derived from the ancient art of Tarot, you might find additional information in a good book emphasizing the **positive** aspects of the Major Arcana cards.

## TAROT LIFETIME AND SPIRITUAL SYMBOLS

### 22 / 0  THE FOOL

Spontaneity
Childlike enthusiasm
Innocence
Trusting the Universe
Fearless
Free
Transcending earthly limits
Finding new ways
Adventuresome
Courageous
Creative vision
Risk taking
Builder of new worlds

*"I boldly step forward."*
*"I walk without fear into new worlds of my boundless, unlimited creation."*
*"All possibilities are open to me as I boundlessly experience the here and now."*


### 1  THE MAGICIAN

Dexterity
Oral and written communication
Commitment
Manifest out of nothing
Self-control
Inspiring
Motivational
Clarity of thought
Desire for honesty
Clear, concise communication
Authentic

*"My thought creates."*
*"The power of my thought and word magically manifest the creation of Spirit."*
*"I am a willing channel for the manifestation of Spirit in the world."*

## 2 THE HIGH PRIESTESS

Deep inner wisdom
Independence
Self-reliance and resourcefulness
Objectivity
Thinking by comparison
Perceptive - quick to see what works and doesn't
Intuitive, psychic
Attunement with own true Self
Seclusion - something hidden
Changeable
Equally male/female, active/receptive, etc.

*"I trust mySelf."*
*"I am my own unlimited resource for self-knowledge, wisdom and the creation of my perfect, balanced expression."*
*"The knowledge that I seek is within myself awaiting my question."*


## 3 THE EMPRESS

Mother Earth
Nurturing
Receptive
Able to equally give and receive love
Fertility, creativity
Happiness
Healer
Lover of beauty
Trusting
Unconditionally loving
A flow of creative thought and action
Seeing the abundance & harmony in everything around

*"I am open to receive all good."*
*"I am nurtured by the unlimited abundance surrounding me as I equally give and receive unconditional love."*
*"I m a fertile garden in which creativity can be nurtured to fruition."*

## 4 THE EMPEROR

Leadership - king, boss
Ambition
Victory
Authority
Confidence
Brings creative vision into worldly manifestation
Power
Desire for excellence
Leadership through integration of body, mind & spirit
Visionary, pioneer
Experiencing wholeness & unity within the Self

*"I see and I create."*
*"I have the confidence and power to manifest my highest visions in practical form for the good of all."*
*"I have the power and discipline to achieve my highest ambitions."*

## 5 THE HIEROPHANT

Counselor, teacher
Healer
Intuitive guidance
Divine wisdom
Expansion of awareness - self & others
Inspirational
Love of Family
Faith in self & others
Grows through teaching/learning experiences
Spiritual discipline
Expansion of awareness
Loyal

*"I am given the wisdom I need."*
*"I trust my higher Self to direct and empower the perfect application of my teaching and inspirational gifts."*
*"I commit my obedience only where and when my Higher Self directs."*

Robert Waldon, ND, PhD

## 6 THE LOVERS

Equal relationships
Synthesis - combining seemingly disparate elements (heart/head, male/female, light/dark, passion/reason, feeling/intellect, etc.)
Knower of the emotional self
Love = Freedom and Trust
Open to inspiration and Divine wisdom
Love in the absence of restrictions
Balancing doing two things
Taking responsibility for choices and actions
Desire to balance giving and receiving
No limits, restrictions or barriers
Sincerity and honesty in relationship

*"I love all unconditionally."*
*"Through giving total freedom and trust I release all apparent polarities and stuckness opening to the perfect experience of love in every relationship."*
*"I choose to be free from inhibition, guild and bondage in all my relationships."*


## 7 THE CHARIOT

Change through decision, conscious choice
Self-discipline
Victory over instincts
Change effecting mental, emotional, physical & spiritual
Freedom and exploration
Successful control of situations
Balance of active and receptive times
Testing what you have learned
Having a sense of direction, a plan
Faithfulness
Following your heart
Confidence, optimism, faith in own abilities

*"I consciously choose for change."*
*"I know my chosen path and consciously focus my energies toward my goal."*
*"By harnessing all my forces toward my purpose and controlling my fears, I victoriously meet my challenges."*

## 8 JUSTICE

Balance, harmony, alignment
Decisions
Desire for completion, resolution
Ability to see both sides
Recognizing the truth about yourself
Clarity
Bringing two aspects of yourself into balance
Equilibrium (self/others, truth/justice, understanding/action, etc.)
Organization, administration
Truth and authenticity
Sense of fair play
Staying centered, listening to the voice within

*"I rest in balance."*
*"I trust my inner sense of justice and impartiality. With truth and authenticity, I express balance and harmony in my life."*
*"I am willing to be true to myself in all my decisions."*


## 9 THE HERMIT

Mastery, completion
Healer
Way-shower, light-bearer (holds the light of inner wisdom & experience)
Honesty and integrity
Illumination from within
Vision quest - a search for something
Abandonment of conventions if favor of inner conviction
Divine inspiration
Transition from completion to initiation
Introspection
Space - physical, emotional or psychic
Order and harmony

*"I know truth in mastery."*
*"I experience mastery of my inner and outer worlds through affirmation of personal conviction and honoring the truth of who I am in all circumstances."*
*"I patiently follow the guidance of my higher Self on the path to enlightenment."*

## 10  WHEEL OF FORTUNE

Success
Finalization & new beginnings
Generosity
Abundance and prosperity
Expansion of life opportunities, opening to the new
Fulfillment
Risking
Optimism - life works
Awakening to possibilities around you
Having a central focus or purpose
Recognizing financial opportunity
Flexible, resilient

*"All abundance is mine."*
*"I open to new opportunities and experience expansion, prosperity and all abundance as I awaken to my inner wholeness."*
*"I rely on the universe to bring me the experiences I need to manifest my full potential."*

## 11  STRENGTH / LUST

Sorting out the valuable
Self-renewal through your creativity and strength
Courage to risk
Endurance
Faith in self
Love as a source of strength
Lust for life - having strong desires and passions
Overcoming old fears with creativity
Control of life forces and driving forces in life
Harnessing natural energy to work in harmony with it
Taming and reigning the beast within
Love without judgment

*"I love all of me."*
*"I am alive, creative, expressive and passionately in love with life and all its opportunities."*
*"I courageously persevere in the loving reconciliation of my lower and higher selves."*

## 12 HANGED MAN

Reversal
Listening to inner self
Freeing self & others from self-imposed limitations
Psychic abilities
Surrender and acceptance
Initiation or transition from one state to another
Deep desire for change
Transformation
Unconventional
Total trust in and surrender to God

*"I surrender to my highest good."*
*"I surrender to the transforming Spirit within, no longer content with old patterns of making myself and others limited and comfortable."*
*"I am willing to suspend my personal comforts for the richness of the spirit."*

## 13 DEATH / REBIRTH

Letting go and getting free
Severance from the past
Becoming more of who we are
Letting go with love and caring
Change of consciousness
Liberation
Renewal
Elimination of the restrictive
Voluntary change
Expansion
Letting go to free self to move ahead
Transformation

*"I let go and am reborn."*
*"I confidently release all which no longer serves my highest good and open to the freedom and expansiveness of my true expression."*
*"I transform and renew myself by letting go of those things no longer necessary to my growth."*

## 14 ART

Recognizing and using available resources
Confidence and enthusiasm
Integration
Blending or combining different aspects in a new way
Synergy
Creative activity
Seeing new possibilities
Outspoken and honest
Open minded
Combining physical and spiritual healing work
Beauty and balance
Communication through creation

*"I know unlimited creation."*
*"I creatively and confidently unite separate elements into new, unique expressions through visioning the many manifestations of wholeness."*
*"I enthusiastically manage my needs and resources to bring about health and harmony."*


## 15  THE DEVIL

Recognizing and transcending inner boundaries
Temptation
Mischievousness
Creativity and innovation
Ambition
Stability in facing seeming problems
Sensual
Following inner joy
Commitment to growth and change
Combining unrelated things in creative new ways
Unaffected by outer judgment
Bringing order out of chaos

*"I am open to new ways."*
*"I recognize no inner restraint as I joyfully follow my heart, opening to new opportunities and experiencing creative solutions to every apparent limitation."*
*"From darkness and chaos I create opportunities to transcend limitations."*

## 16 THE TOWER

Fundamental, basic change
Getting down to the deeper, authentic aspects of self
Breaking down defenses
Destroying the old to make way for the new
Dramatic self-improvement
Desire for more beauty, harmony and authenticity
Being gentle with Self during change
Keenly aware of what is not working in life
Healing through restoration of a more natural state
Breakup, disruption

*"My undoing is my freedom."*
*"I experience deep inner peace in the restoration of what is highest and truest in me and in the destruction and removal of all that is false, restrictive or limiting."*
*"I liberate myself from the ignorance and limitations of old habits and structures whenever I outgrow their need."*

## 17 THE STAR

Inexhaustible inspiration
Self-esteem and confidence
Using active imagination and visualization
Spiritual regeneration
Fully expressive
Charismatic
Altruistic
Living by own truth
Full, open communication
Clarity of vision
Hope
A light in the darkness
Desire to enlighten and raise consciousness of mankind

*"I clearly shine my light."*
*"My radiance, confidence and clarity of vision are shining expressions of who I am, providing light and inspiration for the world."*
*"My inner being shines like a star, guiding my actions, renewing and cleansing me."*

## 18  THE MOON

Voluntary change
Evolution and transformation
Sensitive
Alluring, mysterious
Creates the positive from apparent difficulties
A light in the darkness
Depth of feelings
Impelled from within
Receptive and powerful
Authentic
No tolerance for deception or illusion
Need to flow with feelings

*"I easily flow with my changes."*
*"I choose to support the highest truth and reality through authentic expression of who I am as I change and evolve, coming to know my wholeness."*
*"I am impelled to evolve beyond my fears and insecurities. I am willing to walk the path to self-knowledge through the unknown inner realms of myself."*


## 19  THE SUN

Enlightenment
Manifestation
Creativity and personal growth
Natural generator, motivator, stimulator
Joy, optimism, enthusiasm, vitality
Idealistic
Understanding
Radiates energy, vitality, power
Charismatic
Successful
Overcomes obstacles
Innovative and original

*"I am the light of the world."*
*"I am the source of inspiration, light and joy, bringing clarity and understanding to shared vision and creative exploration."*
*"I create warmth and light with my clarity and enthusiasm."*

## 20 AEON / JUDGMENT

Final decisions concerning the past
Wisdom from experience
Awakening
Sense of purpose
New perceptions, ability to see the whole picture
Learning to see things as they are without judgment
Synthesizing all different aspects of your being
Rebirth, resurrection
Insightful, intuitive
Seeing beyond judgments and criticism
Communicates in inspiring, non-judgmental way
Forgiveness

*"Forgiveness is my road to freedom."*
*"I bring a wealth of wisdom from personal experience to motivate and inspire the re-creation of wholeness in new forms, without evaluation or judgment."*
*"I transform myself daily, awakening yet more to the call of my spirit."*

## 21 THE UNIVERSE

Infinite potential
Full expression of all aspects of Self
Self-actualization
Completion and integration
Totality
Dancing on limitations (using them to free Self & maximize potential)
Innovative
Living comfortably in the midst of complexity
Ability to renew and regenerate self and others
Cutting through limitations
Balanced male/female expression
Taking care of body and the earth to heal both
Manifestation of Spirit on earth

*"I know myself in everything."*
*"I give the totality of my being and my infinite potential to the realization of transformation and the manifestation of Spirit on earth."*
*"The Universe abundantly provides for all my needs."*

## KEYS TO REBALANCING SPIRITUAL SYMBOLS

When you are **on purpose** in your life, you are a balanced expression of the attributes of your Spiritual symbol. When you are **off purpose**, you may tend not to recognize yourself at all in the description of your symbol or to see those attributes as some part of yourself which you vaguely remember from some distant past. You can assist yourself in restoring balance by adopting attributes of a specific other Spiritual symbol.

Below are listed the Spiritual symbols from the Tarot with a short statement of the most obvious or prevalent signs of being off purpose for each symbol. The "assisting" Spiritual symbol and its primary helpful characteristics are given for each. (Expanded information can be found in the book section detailing each Spiritual symbol.)

FOOL — When the Fool becomes fearful or begins to lack trust, he must adopt the characteristics of the **Magician** and begin to manifest, communicate and be inspired.

MAGICIAN — When the Magician begins to fear failure and experience holding back, he must adopt the characteristics of the **Chariot**, taking risks, "going for it" and following what has heart and meaning for him.

HIGH PRIESTESS — When the High Priestess becomes critical and loses faith and trust in her intuition, she must adopt the characteristics of the **Emperor**, exercising her power and leadership, implementing visions and experiencing the wholeness and unity within herself.

EMPRESS — When the Empress finds herself over-giving, pushing, not nurturing herself or sorrowful, he must adopt the characteristics of the **Lovers**, opening to equal relationships, reconciling dualities, opening to inspiration and Divine wisdom and balancing giving and receiving.

EMPEROR — When the Emperor begins following others and stops clearly visioning, he must adopt the characteristics of the **Magician** with his ability to inspire and motivate others and communicate the truth openly and authentically.

HIEROPHANT   When the Hierophant begins to experience worry, fear of defeat, disappointment and holding back, he must adopt the characteristics of **Justice**, opening to balance, truth and authenticity, making decisions and recognizing the truth about himself.

LOVERS   When the Lovers begins to experience poor relationships and trouble with others, he must adopt the characteristics of the **Hermit**, coming to know himself again through introspection, following convictions instead of conventions and expressing honesty and integrity.

CHARIOT   When the Chariot experiences futility, fear of failure, self-indulgence or feeling sorry for himself, he must adopt the characteristics of the **Hierophant**, teaching what he needs to learn, trusting his inner self, creating support systems, engaging in a spiritual discipline and focusing on commitment which joins his heart, mind and action in some cause.

JUSTICE   When Justice begins to doubt or to live out of balance (either indolence or overextension), he must adopt the characteristics of the **High Priestess**, trusting himself, becoming equally dynamic and receptive, objective, self-reliant and quick to see what works and what does not.

HERMIT   When the Hermit begins to indulge in self-cruelty and self-criticalness, he must adopt the characteristics of the **Empress** with her ability to give and receive love, having heart and mind in equal balance, be trusting and receptive and express emotionally.

**Robert Waldon, ND, PhD**

# LIFETIME CYCLES CYCLES OF THE AGES

**Robert Waldon, ND, PhD**

## LIFETIME CYCLES AND CYCLES OF THE AGES

We have looked at the Spiritual Symbol, or Soul Symbol, as representing the Soul's purpose through all of your lifetimes, your "overall" journey. The Lifetime Symbol, or Personality Symbol, represents what you have come into this particular lifetime to learn and can be seen as a "supportive" lesson or an in-depth exploration into a specific aspect of the Spiritual Symbol.

Within each lifetime, there are other groups of "sub-lessons" adding depth or dimension to specific aspects of the lifetime lesson. These are the Lifetime Cycles and they, in turn, are supported by specific lessons of the Personal Year (see next section). We could pursue this further by looking at lessons of Personal Months and Personal Days.

Mastery or completion of any aspect of a lesson learned at the "lowest" level creates a ripple of mastery and change that quickly ascends to the "highest" level of the Soul's overall purpose. Any change at <u>any</u> level in fact creates changes in every level because the Soul "demands" that each level of learning be used for its highest possible purpose in any moment of time.

Looking now at the Lifetime Cycles, they are determined (as described earlier in the book) by the addition of the month and day of birth combined with the current year. Each "decade" marks the beginning of a new Cycle. These cycles are actually 9 years in duration with the 10th year being the "transition" year into the new cycle. Also, each cycle begins with a personal year that is actually the overall symbol for that 10 year period. It gives the energy and sets the overall "tone"

Those with historical or predictive inclinations relative to the world in which we live can apply these cycles to the chronological years of our past or future to get a picture of the evolutionary cycle the world has been following and a possible glimpse into where it is heading. For that reason, there is a brief synopsis of all of the cycles, even though not all apply to our current lifetime, along with a mention of the "transition" year which leads into each cycle.

Remember: If you are looking at "world cycles", you can just consider the year that is given. If you are looking at Lifetime Cycles, the year given will <u>not</u> represent the calendar year you are considering since it is the sum of birth month and day plus the calendar year being considered.

**BUILDER CYCLE**          Begins with #2, High Priestess
Sum = **2000**
Entered through #10 Wheel of Fortune, completions & new beginnings.

This cycle marks a major shift or change in your relationship with the world. Up to this point in time, you have been primarily focusing on learning all the lessons to be learned operating as a physical being in the physical world. This cycle marks the shift into learning all of the different ways for your true Self, your higher Spiritual Self to relate to the world and express in the world. It's the beginning of expressing Spirit in the world and will be a period of trial and error, thinking by comparison, lots of changes, discovering what's hidden and the development of self-reliance.

**PATH OF THE HEART**          Begins with #3, The Empress
Sum = **2010**
Entered through #11 Strength/Lust, sorting out the valuable, love without judgment.
Sum = **2100**
Entered through #20 Aeon/Judgment, total forgiveness.

Finding out what has heart and meaning and pleasure, what nurtures and supports you. Exploration of emotions, very receptive time. Creativity, beauty and happiness become more of a focus. No tolerance for anything that you "should" do but which doesn't nurture or inspire you.

**PATH OF LEADERSHIP**          Begins with #4, The Emperor
Sum = **2020** and **2110**
Entered through #12 The Hanged Man, total trust in and surrender to God
Sum = **2200**
Entered through #21 The Universe, Self-actualization, manifesting Spirit on Earth.

Acting on your dreams and visions and experiencing your wholeness in action. A time to develop and demonstrate your power, authority, confidence and leadership. Bringing your visions into manifestation in the world, empowering self and others.

**PATH OF SUCCESS**          Begins with #5, The Hierophant
Sum = **2030** and **2120** and **2210**
Entered through #13 Death/Rebirth, eliminating restrictive, severance from past, change of consciousness.

Previous efforts acknowledged with success as we become the teacher/ student. Divine wisdom, intuitive guidance, healing through knowing and seeing wholeness. Spiritual development.

**PATH OF LOVE**                    Begins with #6, The Lovers
Sum = **2040** and **2130** and **2220**
Entered through #14 Art, creative expression, total honesty and openness,
Spiritual healing.

Learning about and experiencing equal relationships. Creating through full
expression. Experiencing unconditional love, love in the absence of restrictions.

**PATH OF FREEDOM**                 Begins with #7, The Chariot
Sum = **2050** and **2140** and **2230**
Entered through #15 The Devil, transcending inner restrictions, seeing yourself
in a new, creative way.

Following your own chosen path and direction. Spiritual exploration and
freedom. Taking responsibility for your creations and consciously choosing for
what you want.

**PATH OF HARMONY**                 Begins with #8, Justice
Sum = **2060** and **2150** and **2240**
Entered through #16 The Tower, breaking down all defenses, eliminating all
restrictions, doing away with the old and outmoded.

Knowing that we are one with the universe and giving what we want to receive.
Recognizing the truth about ourselves through simplification and balance.

**PATH OF ENLIGHTENMENT**           Begins with #9, The Hermit
Sum = **2070** and **2160** and **2250**
Entered through #17 The Star, spiritual regeneration, full and open
communication, use of imagination and visualization to raise consciousness of
mankind. Peace.

Knowing we are one with God and seeing the world through that Light.
Mastery, completion. Holding the highest vision. Illumination from within.

**PATH OF FULFILLMENT**             Begins with #10, Wheel of Fortune
Sum = **2080** and **2170** and **2260**
Entered through #18 The Moon, full self-knowledge, discovering the depths of
you being, end of fear and insecurity.

Taking the full expression of your being to a higher level of consciousness. To
give all is to have all. Success, finalization and new beginnings.

**PATH OF STRENGTH**          Begins with #11, Strength/Lust
Sum = **2090** and **2180** and **2270**
Entered through #19 The Sun, overcoming all obstacles, wisdom,
enlightenment, manifestation.

Drawing unlimited strength from the Divine.  Not relying on personal power.
Love as a source of strength.  Courage to risk acting on highest desires.

**PATH OF TRANSITION**          Begins with #12, Hanged Man
Sum = **2190**
Entered through #20 Aeon/Judgment, final decisions about the past, synthesis
of all aspects of your being, total forgiveness.

Total trust in and surrender to God.  The end of sacrifice.  Living your divinity.

**PATH OF TRANSFORMATION**          Begins with #13, Death/Rebirth
Sum = **2290**
Entered through #21 The World, self-actualization, manifesting Spirit on Earth,
total healing of bodies and the earth.

Eliminating restrictive forms, voluntary change of consciousness, dropping and
assuming bodily form at will.

**PATH OF ART**          Begins with #14, Art
Sum = **1940**
Entered through #4 The Emperor, taking action on new things, leadership,
authority, power and confidence.

Recognizing and using available resources.  Blending and combining different
aspects in new ways.  Confidence and enthusiasm.

**PATH OF INNOVATION**          Begins with #15, The Devil
Sum = **1950**
Entered through #5 The Hierophant, intuitive guidance, counseling,
teaching/learning, spiritual discipline.

Recognizing and transcending inner boundaries.  Bringing order out of chaos.
Combining unrelated things in new, creative ways.  Innovation.

## PATH OF CHANGE                    Begins with #16, The Tower
Sum = **1960**

Entered through #6 The Lovers, synthesis, combining elements, taking responsibility for choices and actions.

Self-improvement. Fundamental, basic, change. Disruption and dismantling old forms to make way for the new. Desire to bring things into a state of more beauty and harmony.

## PATH OF INSPIRATION              Begins with #17, The Star
Sum = **1970**

Entered through #7 The Chariot, faith in own abilities, having a sense of direction or plan, freedom and exploration.

Spiritual awakening (rebirth), living by own truth and full, open communication.

## PATH OF SELF-KNOWLEDGE           Begins with #18, The Moon
Sum = **1980**

Entered through #8 Justice, seeing both sides, balance, harmony, recognizing the truth about self.

Looking into or discovering the depths of the inner being. Flowing with feelings. Voluntary change. Evolution, transformation. Exploring new worlds.

## PATH OF CREATIVITY               Begins with #19, The Sun
Sum = **1990**

Entered through #9 The Hermit, abandonment of conventions thorough inner conviction, introspection.

Creativity and personal growth. Overcoming obstacles. Enlightenment and clarity. The "success" cycle of the physical world expression.

## PATH OF AWAKENING                Begins with #20, Aeon
Sum = **1910**

Entered through #19 The Sun, clarity, overcoming obstacles.

Awakening of new perceptions. Sense of purpose. Final decisions concerning the past. Learning to see things as they are without judgment.

## PATH OF ABUNDANCE                Begins with #21, Universe
Entered through #20 Aeon, new perceptions, end of self-criticism, synthesizing different aspects of your being.

Overcoming limitations and realizing that everything is available to you. Building new worlds (inner and outer). Actualization of potential.

## PARTIAL CHRONOLOGICAL LISTING OF CYCLES

| YEAR | CYCLE |
|------|-------|
| 1900 | FULFILLMENT - 10 |
| 1910 | STRENGTH - 11 |
| 1920 | TRANSITION - 12 |
| 1930 | TRANSFORMATION - 13 |
| 1940 | ART - 14 |
| 1950 | INNOVATION - 15 |
| 1960 | CHANGE - 16 |
| 1970 | INSPIRATION - 17 |
| 1980 | SELF-KNOWLEDGE - 18 |
| 1990 | CREATIVITY - 19 |
| 2000 | BUILDER - 2 (1st & last, age of Aquarius) |
| 2010 | HEART - 3 |
| 2020 | LEADERSHIP - 4 |
| 2030 | SUCCESS - 5 |
| 2040 | LOVE - 6 |
| 2050 | FREEDOM - 7 |
| 2060 | HARMONY - 8 |
| 2070 | ENLIGHTENMENT - 9 |
| 2080 | FULFILLMENT - 10 |
| 2090 | STRENGTH - 11 |
| 2100 | HEART - 3 (last for a while) |
| 2110 | LEADERSHIP - 4 |
| 2120 | SUCCESS - 5 |
| 2130 | LOVE - 6 |
| 2140 | FREEDOM - 7 |
| 2150 | HARMONY - 8 |
| 2160 | ENLIGHTENMENT - 9 |
| 2170 | FULFILLMENT - 10 |
| 2180 | STRENGTH - 11 |
| 2190 | TRANSITION - 12 (back in again) |
| 2200 | LEADERSHIP - 4 (last) 22=BUILDER OF NEW WORLDS |
| 2210 | SUCCESS - 5 |
| 2220 | LOVE - 6 |
| 2230 | FREEDOM - 7 |
| 2240 | HARMONY - 8 |
| 2250 | ENLIGHTENMENT - 9 |
| 2260 | FULFILLMENT - 10 |
| 2270 | STRENGTH - 11 |
| 2280 | TRANSITION - 12 |
| 2290 | TRANSFORMATION - 13 (back in again) |
| 2300 | SUCCESS - 5 |

Robert Waldon, ND, PhD

| YEAR | # | CYCLE | YEAR | # | CYCLE |
|------|---|-------|------|---|-------|
| 1800 | 9 | ENLIGHTENMENT | 1850 | 14 | ART |
| 1801 | 10 | | 1851 | 15 | |
| 1802 | 11 | | 1852 | 16 | |
| 1803 | 12 | | 1853 | 17 | |
| 1804 | 13 | | 1854 | 18 | |
| 1805 | 14 | | 1855 | 19 | |
| 1806 | 15 | | 1856 | 20 | |
| 1807 | 16 | | 1857 | 21 | |
| 1808 | 17 | | 1858 | 22 | |
| 1809 | 18 | | 1859 | 5 | |
| 1810 | 10 | FULFILLMENT | 1860 | 15 | INNOVATION |
| 1811 | 11 | | 1861 | 16 | |
| 1812 | 12 | | 1862 | 17 | |
| 1813 | 13 | | 1863 | 18 | |
| 1814 | 14 | | 1864 | 19 | |
| 1815 | 15 | | 1865 | 20 | |
| 1816 | 16 | | 1866 | 21 | |
| 1817 | 17 | | 1867 | 22 | |
| 1818 | 18 | | 1868 | 5 | |
| 1819 | 19 | | 1869 | 6 | |
| 1820 | 11 | STRENGTH | 1870 | 16 | CHANGE |
| 1821 | 12 | | 1871 | 17 | |
| 1822 | 13 | | 1872 | 18 | |
| 1823 | 14 | | 1873 | 19 | |
| 1824 | 15 | | 1874 | 20 | |
| 1825 | 16 | | 1875 | 21 | |
| 1826 | 17 | | 1876 | 22 | |
| 1827 | 18 | | 1877 | 5 | |
| 1828 | 19 | | 1878 | 6 | |
| 1829 | 20 | | 1879 | 7 | |
| 1830 | 12 | TRANSITION | 1880 | 17 | INSPIRATION |
| 1831 | 13 | | 1881 | 18 | |
| 1832 | 14 | | 1882 | 19 | |
| 1833 | 15 | | 1883 | 20 | |
| 1834 | 16 | | 1884 | 21 | |
| 1835 | 17 | | 1885 | 22 | |
| 1836 | 18 | | 1886 | 5 | |
| 1837 | 19 | | 1887 | 6 | |
| 1838 | 20 | | 1888 | 7 | |
| 1839 | 21 | | 1889 | 8 | |
| 1840 | 13 | TRANSFORMATION | 1890 | 18 | SELF- |
| KNOWLEDGE | | | | | |
| 1841 | 14 | | 1891 | 19 | |
| 1842 | 15 | | 1892 | 20 | |
| 1843 | 16 | | 1893 | 21 | |
| 1844 | 17 | | 1894 | 22 | |
| 1845 | 18 | | 1895 | 5 | |
| 1846 | 19 | | 1896 | 6 | |
| 1847 | 20 | | 1897 | 7 | |
| 1848 | 21 | | 1898 | 8 | |
| 1849 | 22 | | 1899 | 9 | |

| YEAR | # | CYCLE | YEAR | # | CYCLE |
|---|---|---|---|---|---|
| 1900 | 10 | FULFILLMENT | 1950 | 15 | INNOVATION |
| 1901 | 11 | | 1951 | 16 | |
| 1902 | 12 | | 1952 | 17 | |
| 1903 | 13 | | 1953 | 18 | |
| 1904 | 14 | | 1954 | 19 | |
| 1905 | 15 | | 1955 | 20 | |
| 1906 | 16 | | 1956 | 21 | |
| 1907 | 17 | | 1957 | 22 | |
| 1908 | 18 | | 1958 | 5 | |
| 1909 | 19 | | 1959 | 6 | |
| 1910 | 11 | STRENGTH | 1960 | 16 | CHANGE |
| 1911 | 12 | | 1961 | 17 | |
| 1912 | 13 | | 1962 | 18 | |
| 1913 | 14 | | 1963 | 19 | |
| 1914 | 15 | | 1964 | 20 | |
| 1915 | 16 | | 1965 | 21 | |
| 1916 | 17 | | 1966 | 22 | |
| 1917 | 18 | | 1967 | 5 | |
| 1918 | 19 | | 1968 | 6 | |
| 1919 | 20 | | 1969 | 7 | |
| 1920 | 12 | TRANSITION | 1970 | 17 | INSPIRATION |
| 1921 | 13 | | 1971 | 18 | |
| 1922 | 14 | | 1972 | 19 | |
| 1923 | 15 | | 1973 | 20 | |
| 1924 | 16 | | 1974 | 21 | |
| 1925 | 17 | | 1975 | 22 | |
| 1926 | 18 | | 1976 | 5 | |
| 1927 | 19 | | 1977 | 6 | |
| 1928 | 20 | | 1978 | 7 | |
| 1929 | 21 | | 1979 | 8 | |
| 1930 | 13 | TRANSFORMATION | 1980 | 18 | SELF- |
| KNOWLEDGE | | | | | |
| 1931 | 14 | | 1981 | 19 | |
| 1932 | 15 | | 1982 | 20 | |
| 1933 | 16 | | 1983 | 21 | |
| 1934 | 17 | | 1984 | 22 | |
| 1935 | 18 | | 1985 | 5 | |
| 1936 | 19 | | 1986 | 6 | |
| 1937 | 20 | | 1987 | 7 | |
| 1938 | 21 | | 1988 | 8 | |
| 1939 | 22 | | 1989 | 9 | |
| 1940 | 14 | ART | 1990 | 19 | CREATIVITY |
| 1941 | 15 | | 1991 | 20 | |
| 1942 | 16 | | 1992 | 21 | |
| 1943 | 17 | | 1993 | 22 | |
| 1944 | 18 | | 1994 | 5 | |
| 1945 | 19 | | 1995 | 6 | |
| 1946 | 20 | | 1996 | 7 | |
| 1947 | 21 | | 1997 | 8 | |
| 1948 | 22 | | 1998 | 9 | |
| 1949 | 5 | | 1999 | 10 | |

| YEAR | # | CYCLE | YEAR | # | CYCLE |
|------|---|-------|------|---|-------|
| 2000 | 2 | BUILDER | 2050 | 7 | FREEDOM |
| 2001 | 3 | | 2051 | 8 | |
| 2002 | 4 | | 2052 | 9 | |
| 2003 | 5 | | 2053 | 10 | |
| 2004 | 6 | | 2054 | 11 | |
| 2005 | 7 | | 2055 | 12 | |
| 2006 | 8 | | 2056 | 13 | |
| 2007 | 9 | | 2057 | 14 | |
| 2008 | 10 | | 2058 | 15 | |
| 2009 | 11 | | 2059 | 16 | |
| 2010 | 3 | HEART | 2060 | 8 | HARMONY |
| 2011 | 4 | | 2061 | 9 | |
| 2012 | 5 | | 2062 | 10 | |
| 2013 | 6 | | 2063 | 11 | |
| 2014 | 7 | | 2064 | 12 | |
| 2015 | 8 | | 2065 | 13 | |
| 2016 | 9 | | 2066 | 14 | |
| 2017 | 10 | | 2067 | 15 | |
| 2018 | 11 | | 2068 | 16 | |
| 2019 | 12 | | 2069 | 17 | |
| 2020 | 4 | LEADERSHIP ENLIGHTENMENT | 2070 | 9 | |
| 2021 | 5 | | 2071 | 10 | |
| 2022 | 6 | | 2072 | 11 | |
| 2023 | 7 | | 2073 | 12 | |
| 2024 | 8 | | 2074 | 13 | |
| 2025 | 9 | | 2075 | 14 | |
| 2026 | 10 | | 2076 | 15 | |
| 2027 | 11 | | 2077 | 16 | |
| 2028 | 12 | | 2078 | 17 | |
| 2029 | 13 | | 2079 | 18 | |
| 2030 | 5 | SUCCESS | 2080 | 10 | FULFILLMENT |
| 2031 | 6 | | 2081 | 11 | |
| 2032 | 7 | | 2082 | 12 | |
| 2033 | 8 | | 2083 | 13 | |
| 2034 | 9 | | 2084 | 14 | |
| 2035 | 10 | | 2085 | 15 | |
| 2036 | 11 | | 2086 | 16 | |
| 2037 | 12 | | 2087 | 17 | |
| 2038 | 13 | | 2088 | 18 | |
| 2039 | 14 | | 2089 | 19 | |
| 2040 | 6 | LOVE | 2090 | 11 | STRENGTH |
| 2041 | 7 | | 2091 | 12 | |
| 2042 | 8 | | 2092 | 13 | |
| 2043 | 9 | | 2093 | 14 | |
| 2044 | 10 | | 2094 | 15 | |
| 2045 | 11 | | 2095 | 16 | |
| 2046 | 12 | | 2096 | 17 | |
| 2047 | 13 | | 2097 | 18 | |
| 2048 | 14 | | 2098 | 19 | |
| 2049 | 15 | | 2099 | 20 | |

| YEAR | # | CYCLE | YEAR | # | CYCLE |
|------|---|-------|------|---|-------|
| 2100 | 3 | HEART | 2150 | 8 | HARMONY |
| 2101 | 4 | | 2151 | 9 | |
| 2102 | 5 | | 2152 | 10 | |
| 2103 | 6 | | 2153 | 11 | |
| 2104 | 7 | | 2154 | 12 | |
| 2105 | 8 | | 2155 | 13 | |
| 2106 | 9 | | 2156 | 14 | |
| 2107 | 10 | | 2157 | 15 | |
| 2108 | 11 | | 2158 | 16 | |
| 2109 | 12 | | 2159 | 17 | |
| 2110 | 4 | LEADERSHIP ENLIGHTENMENT | 2160 | 9 | |
| 2111 | 5 | | 2161 | 10 | |
| 2112 | 6 | | 2162 | 11 | |
| 2113 | 7 | | 2163 | 12 | |
| 2114 | 8 | | 2164 | 13 | |
| 2115 | 9 | | 2165 | 14 | |
| 2116 | 10 | | 2166 | 15 | |
| 2117 | 11 | | 2167 | 16 | |
| 2118 | 12 | | 2168 | 17 | |
| 2119 | 13 | | 2169 | 18 | |
| 2120 | 5 | SUCCESS | 2170 | 10 | FULFILLMENT |
| 2121 | 6 | | 2171 | 11 | |
| 2122 | 7 | | 2172 | 12 | |
| 2123 | 8 | | 2173 | 13 | |
| 2124 | 9 | | 2174 | 14 | |
| 2125 | 10 | | 2175 | 15 | |
| 2126 | 11 | | 2176 | 16 | |
| 2127 | 12 | | 2177 | 17 | |
| 2128 | 13 | | 2178 | 18 | |
| 2129 | 14 | | 2179 | 19 | |
| 2130 | 6 | LOVE | 2180 | 11 | STRENGTH |
| 2131 | 7 | | 2181 | 12 | |
| 2132 | 8 | | 2182 | 13 | |
| 2133 | 9 | | 2183 | 14 | |
| 2134 | 10 | | 2184 | 15 | |
| 2135 | 11 | | 2185 | 16 | |
| 2136 | 12 | | 2186 | 17 | |
| 2137 | 13 | | 2187 | 18 | |
| 2138 | 14 | | 2188 | 19 | |
| 2139 | 15 | | 2189 | 20 | |
| 2140 | 7 | FREEDOM | 2190 | 12 | TRANSITION |
| 2141 | 8 | | 2191 | 13 | |
| 2142 | 9 | | 2192 | 14 | |
| 2143 | 10 | | 2193 | 15 | |
| 2144 | 11 | | 2194 | 16 | |
| 2145 | 12 | | 2195 | 17 | |
| 2146 | 13 | | 2196 | 18 | |
| 2147 | 14 | | 2197 | 19 | |
| 2148 | 15 | | 2198 | 20 | |
| 2149 | 16 | | 2199 | 21 | |

**Robert Waldon, ND, PhD**

| YEAR | # | CYCLE | YEAR | # | CYCLE |
|------|----|--------------|------|----|----------------|
| 2200 | 4 | LEADERSHIP ENLIGHTENMENT | 2250 | 9 | |
| 2201 | 5 | | 2251 | 10 | |
| 2202 | 6 | | 2252 | 11 | |
| 2203 | 7 | | 2253 | 12 | |
| 2204 | 8 | | 2254 | 13 | |
| 2205 | 9 | | 2255 | 14 | |
| 2206 | 10 | | 2256 | 15 | |
| 2207 | 11 | | 2257 | 16 | |
| 2208 | 12 | | 2258 | 17 | |
| 2209 | 13 | | 2259 | 18 | |
| 2210 | 5 | SUCCESS | 2260 | 10 | FULFILLMENT |
| 2211 | 6 | | 2261 | 11 | |
| 2212 | 7 | | 2262 | 12 | |
| 2213 | 8 | | 2263 | 13 | |
| 2214 | 9 | | 2264 | 14 | |
| 2215 | 10 | | 2265 | 15 | |
| 2216 | 11 | | 2266 | 16 | |
| 2217 | 12 | | 2267 | 17 | |
| 2218 | 13 | | 2268 | 18 | |
| 2219 | 14 | | 2269 | 19 | |
| 2220 | 6 | LOVE | 2270 | 11 | STRENGTH |
| 2221 | 7 | | 2271 | 12 | |
| 2222 | 8 | | 2272 | 13 | |
| 2223 | 9 | | 2273 | 14 | |
| 2224 | 10 | | 2274 | 15 | |
| 2225 | 11 | | 2275 | 16 | |
| 2226 | 12 | | 2276 | 17 | |
| 2227 | 13 | | 2277 | 18 | |
| 2228 | 14 | | 2278 | 19 | |
| 2229 | 15 | | 2279 | 20 | |
| 2230 | 7 | FREEDOM | 2280 | 12 | TRANSITION |
| 2231 | 8 | | 2281 | 13 | |
| 2232 | 9 | | 2282 | 14 | |
| 2233 | 10 | | 2283 | 15 | |
| 2234 | 11 | | 2284 | 16 | |
| 2235 | 12 | | 2285 | 17 | |
| 2236 | 13 | | 2286 | 18 | |
| 2237 | 14 | | 2287 | 19 | |
| 2238 | 15 | | 2288 | 20 | |
| 2239 | 16 | | 2289 | 21 | |
| 2240 | 8 | HARMONY | 2290 | 13 | TRANSFORMATION |
| 2241 | 9 | | 2291 | 14 | |
| 2242 | 10 | | 2292 | 15 | |
| 2243 | 11 | | 2293 | 16 | |
| 2244 | 12 | | 2294 | 17 | |
| 2245 | 13 | | 2295 | 18 | |
| 2246 | 14 | | 2296 | 19 | |
| 2247 | 15 | | 2297 | 20 | |
| 2248 | 16 | | 2298 | 21 | |
| 2249 | 17 | | 2299 | 22 | |

| YEAR | # | CYCLE | YEAR | # | CYCLE |
|------|---|-------|------|---|-------|
| 2300 | 5 | SUCCESS | 2350 | 10 | FULFILLMENT |
| 2301 | 6 | | 2351 | 11 | |
| 2302 | 7 | | 2352 | 12 | |
| 2303 | 8 | | 2353 | 13 | |
| 2304 | 9 | | 2354 | 14 | |
| 2305 | 10 | | 2355 | 15 | |
| 2306 | 11 | | 2356 | 16 | |
| 2307 | 12 | | 2357 | 17 | |
| 2308 | 13 | | 2358 | 18 | |
| 2309 | 14 | | 2359 | 19 | |
| 2310 | 6 | LOVE | 2360 | 11 | STRENGTH |
| 2311 | 7 | | 2361 | 12 | |
| 2312 | 8 | | 2362 | 13 | |
| 2313 | 9 | | 2363 | 14 | |
| 2314 | 10 | | 2364 | 15 | |
| 2315 | 11 | | 2365 | 16 | |
| 2316 | 12 | | 2366 | 17 | |
| 2317 | 13 | | 2367 | 18 | |
| 2318 | 14 | | 2368 | 19 | |
| 2319 | 15 | | 2369 | 20 | |
| 2320 | 7 | FREEDOM | 2370 | 12 | TRANSITION |
| 2321 | 8 | | 2371 | 13 | |
| 2322 | 9 | | 2372 | 14 | |
| 2323 | 10 | | 2373 | 15 | |
| 2324 | 11 | | 2374 | 16 | |
| 2325 | 12 | | 2375 | 17 | |
| 2326 | 13 | | 2376 | 18 | |
| 2327 | 14 | | 2377 | 19 | |
| 2328 | 15 | | 2378 | 20 | |
| 2329 | 16 | | 2379 | 21 | |
| 2330 | 8 | HARMONY | 2380 | 13 | TRANSFORMATION |
| 2331 | 9 | | 2381 | 14 | |
| 2332 | 10 | | 2382 | 15 | |
| 2333 | 11 | | 2383 | 16 | |
| 2334 | 12 | | 2384 | 17 | |
| 2335 | 13 | | 2385 | 18 | |
| 2336 | 14 | | 2386 | 19 | |
| 2337 | 15 | | 2387 | 20 | |
| 2338 | 16 | | 2388 | 21 | |
| 2339 | 17 | | 2389 | 22 | |
| 2340 | 9 | ENLIGHTENMENT | 2390 | 14 | ART |
| 2341 | 10 | | 2391 | 15 | |
| 2342 | 11 | | 2392 | 16 | |
| 2343 | 12 | | 2393 | 17 | |
| 2344 | 13 | | 2394 | 18 | |
| 2345 | 14 | | 2395 | 19 | |
| 2346 | 15 | | 2396 | 20 | |
| 2347 | 16 | | 2397 | 21 | |
| 2348 | 17 | | 2398 | 22 | |
| 2349 | 18 | | 2399 | 5 | |

Robert Waldon, ND, PhD

# UNIVERSAL AND PERSONAL YEAR SYMBOLS

## UNIVERSAL AND PERSONAL YEAR SYMBOLS

(Note: **Additional information should be gathered** by referring to the previous section on Lifetime symbols and their explanations.)
There is no Fool or Magician personal or universal year.

### 2 Year **THE HIGH PRIESTESS**

A time to evaluate who one is and is not. Develop trust, independence, resourcefulness and perception. Emergence of new identity. No tolerance for limits, restrictions and restraints. Need to be on your own. Trust your intuition and learn to control any attitudes of criticalness.

*"I trust mySelf"*
*"I am my own unlimited resource for self-knowledge, wisdom and the creation of my perfect, balanced expression."*

### 3 Year **THE EMPRESS**

Clarify what is emotionally important and what is not. Resolve mother issues. Bring more beauty, harmony and nature into one's life. Nurture and support yourself as well as others. Don't over-give or push to create changes.

*"I am open to receive all good."*
*"I am nurtured by the unlimited abundance surrounding me as I equally give and receive unconditional love."*

### 4 Year **THE EMPEROR**

Experience leadership. Move or relocate. Father issues. Start new projects, move in new directions where you can own your own power and leadership. Be willing to have expansive vision and put your ideals and visions into form.

*"I see and I create."*
*"I have the confidence and power to manifest my highest visions in practical form for the good of all."*

### 5 Year **THE HIEROPHANT**

Resolve family issues, breaking old family patterns and conditioning. Desire to go back to school or to train in some new field. Wanting to teach, counsel or consult with others. Internal growth and development. Don't restrain yourself and don't worry about what you are doing. Release all past disappointment and failure.

*"I am given the wisdom I need."*
*"I trust my higher Self to direct and empower the perfect application of my teaching and inspirational gifts."*

## 6 Year **THE LOVERS**

Reassess relationships. A choice-making year, weighing two choices or options. Support only equal relationships. Decisions and choices regarding support systems. Personally model in your life the type of relationships you desire and perfect your abilities to work with others.

*"I love all unconditionally."*
*"Through giving total freedom and trust, I release all apparent polarities and stuckness, opening to the perfect experience of love in every relationship."*

## 7 Year **THE CHARIOT**

Move, relocate, travel. Possible career changes. Positive, expansive changes. Make changes that nurture and support you. Take control of your life and take responsibility for consciously choosing. Take positive action to avoid any fear of failure. Don't feel sorry for yourself, but take positive steps to change the circumstances.

*"I consciously choose for change."*
*"I know my chosen path and consciously focus my energies toward my goal."*

## 8 Year **JUSTICE**

Bring your life back into balance. Simplify your life, create clarity, order and harmony. Utilize your ideas in a practical way. Focus on truth and authenticity. A time of healing, making whole. Don't go too far from "center" with any project and don't let self-doubt or doubts from others interfere with what you know is best.

*"I rest in balance."*
*"I trust my inner sense of justice and impartiality. With truth and authenticity, I express balance and harmony in my life."*

## 9 Year **THE HERMIT**

Complete any unfinished business from the past. A time for contemplation, perhaps with periods of retreat and silence. You may be called out to lead, inspire or motivate others. A year to clear up any areas of self-cruelty or criticalness in your life.

*"I know truth in mastery."*
*"I experience mastery of my inner and outer worlds through affirmation of personal conviction and honoring the truth of who I am in all circumstances.*

## 10 Year **WHEEL OF FORTUNE**
Positive changes of direction and fortune. Unexpected opportunities. Be open to abundance in all areas of your life and get un-stuck from old habits and ways of doing things. Be flexible, non-judgmental and open to good fortune. A year to fully express original ideas and visions.

*"All abundance is mine."*
*"I open to new opportunities and experience expansion, prosperity and all abundance as I awaken to my inner wholeness."*

## 11 Year **STRENGTH / LUST**
Renewed energy, lust and passion for all areas of life. Getting free from old fears and confronting the hidden parts of yourself (taming and reigning the beast within). Become more fully who you are by tapping into your inner resources of strength. A year to be willing to be strong and express strongly.

*"I love all of me."*
*"I am alive, creative, expressive and passionately in love with life and all its opportunities."*

## 12 Year **HANGED MAN**
Breaking destructive, limiting patterns and habits in your life. Coming up against historical patterns of limitation. Be open to see the love in all events and surrender to your higher Spiritual nature. A year to carefully examine your motives for any sacrifices you are or have been making and to stop sacrificing just to make yourself or others more comfortable.

*"I surrender to my highest good."*
*"I surrender to the transforming Spirit within, no longer content with old patterns of making myself and others limited and comfortable."*

## 13 Year **DEATH / REBIRTH**
Death of old parts of yourself, of old identities which no longer serve you. The end of some project or relationship and an opening up to something new. Letting go of unnecessary attachments to give birth to new experiences and new aspects of yourself. A year to learn about letting go with love, caring and compassion.

*"I let go and am reborn."*
*"I confidently release all which no longer serves my highest good and open to the freedom and expansiveness of my true expression."*

## 14 Year **ART**

New artistic creations, new combinations of people or things in your life bringing more balance and beauty. Things start to fall into place, to make some sense as you resolve seeming polarities and paradoxes in your experience. A year to release any lingering disappointment, worry or anxiety and be free to create anew.

*"I know unlimited creation."*
*"I creatively and confidently unite separate elements into new, unique expressions through visioning the many manifestations of wholeness."*

## 15 Year **THE DEVIL**

Maintain your sense of humor, regardless of events. Don't take life too seriously. Maintain a sense of "center", perspective or balance. Creative ideas and energy will begin to flow. You may deal with areas of comfort relating to body and sensuality. Your creativity will find a way through the seriousness which appears to confront you and turn them to humor.

*"I am open to new ways."*
*"I recognize no inner restraint as I joyfully follow my heart, opening to new opportunities and experiencing creative solutions to every apparent limitation."*

## 16 Year **THE TOWER**

A year to break away from old patterns, to shed outdated roles, people, places or things as you seek to experience an alignment of your inner being with your creation in the outer world. Through tearing down the old you will come to a greater awareness of who you really are. You may undertake personal "renovation" through diet, exercise, meditation, etc. A year to release past feelings of futility and fears of failure and be willing to succeed in your life.

*"My undoing is my freedom."*
*"I experience deep inner peace in the restoration of what is highest and truest in me and in the destruction and removal of all that is false, restrictive or limiting."*

## 17 Year **THE STAR**

Building of true self-esteem and self-confidence and the release of any need to "create an image" for others, to either inflate or deflate yourself or another. You may awaken to a new self-trust, self-sufficiency and self-respect. It's a time to release any lingering self-doubts which have inhibited you in the past.

*"I clearly shine my light."*
*"My radiance, confidence and clarity of vision are shining expressions of who I am, providing light and inspiration for the world."*

## 18 Year **THE MOON**
A year to become comfortable authentically expressing all of your feelings and emotions, to fully "own" the depth of feelings which you have. Intolerance for any illusions, delusions, self-deceptions. Choosing to honor, support and be your true Self under all circumstances. A year of opening up and letting go of past frustration at not being fully know by others.

*"I easily flow with my changes."*
*"I choose to support the highest truth and reality through authentic expression of who I am as I change and evolve, coming to know my wholeness."*

## 19 Year **THE SUN**
A year to connect with people, opportunities and situations which inspire you and bring out your aliveness and vitality. A good time for inspirational joinings and to remove yourself from relationships which drain you or do not fully support you. A year to totally go for it and be willing to be fully who you are.

*"I am the light of the world."*
*"I am the source of inspiration, light and joy, bringing clarity and understanding to shared vision and creative exploration."*

## 20 Year **AEON / JUDGMENT**
Be open to new activities and areas of interest in both your personal and your professional life. A good time to work with close family members, close friends or loved ones on creative projects. Be willing to communicate fully and learn to share your perceptions and ideas clearly and without judgment. Transform any tendency to be critical through forgiveness and seeing things differently.

*"Forgiveness is my road to freedom."*
*"I bring a wealth of wisdom from personal experience to motivate and inspire the re-creation of wholeness in new forms, without evaluation or judgment."*

## 21 Year **THE UNIVERSE**
A strong draw to becoming more complete in your experience of yourself and in the expression of you full self to others. Become actively involved in your world. You can see clearly what needs to be done and now is the time to do it. It is a year to follow your heart and you will have little tolerance for "shoulds". Release all past sadness by active involvement.

*"I know myself in everything."*
*"I give the totality of my being and my infinite potential to the realization of transformation and the manifestation of Spirit on earth."*

# THE SPIRITUAL
# BODIES

## THE SPIRITUAL BODIES

There are ten spiritual or subtle bodies at work in your life related to your specific work here on earth. Each is briefly described below along with a sample affirmation to strengthen your awareness and bring more aliveness to this aspect of your being.

1    The **Soul**, representing creativity and humility.
*"I am perfectly led by my heart."*
*"I totally trust and follow the guidance of my heart in all that I think, say and do."*

2    The **Negative Mind**, representing the part of ourselves which calculates danger (to body or soul) as well as our devotion, our longing to belong.
*"My devotion to God is all."*
*"I am devoted only to the Spirit of Love in each relationship, letting all other fears, needs and dependencies drop away."*

3    The **Positive Mind**, the part of us which sees opportunities and benefits and is concerned with equality and humanitarian ideals.
*"I see good and know it."*
*"I see the good in all people and events, opening me to unlimited opportunities and the experience of abundance for All."*

4    The **Neutral Mind**, the mind of service. The Neutral Mind takes information from the Positive Mind (all the good, what we want, etc.) and from the Negative Mind (the potential problems, fears, avoidances, etc.) and chooses based on what is truly in the best interests of everyone involved.
*"I serve only the truest call."*
*"I set aside all fears and desires coming from myself and others and respond only to support the highest and best for all concerned."*

5    The **Physical Body**, representing balance and teaching by example.
*"I live the lessons I would teach."*
*"I learn from every life experience, choosing only for my highest good and teaching others by my living example of truth and integrity."*

6    The **Third Eye** (or Spiritual Eye), representing focused attention and intuition and justice.
*"My focus is my power."*
*"I experience the manifested power of my every thought and word as my natural focus creates a concentration of Spirit-filled energy."*

7        The **Aura**, representing the ability to uplift, a strong self-identity, peace and mercy.
*"I am inspired as I inspire."*
*"My presence alone is a blessing to all, bringing inspiration, peace and enlightenment."*

8        **Prana** (the life energy in breath), representing purity and healing and strongly expressed in music and singing.
*"In my love is all healed."*
*"I am the breath of God, bringing life and wholeness to all with the purity of my loving energy."*

9        The **Subtle Body**, representing mastery, steadfastness and calmness.
*"I am calm, knowing mastery of Self."*
*"I am peaceful, gentle and calm, knowing that strength and protection are found within mastery of the Self."*

10      The **Radiant Body**, representing the radiance of the Soul, the visionary, royal courage.
*"I hold to my true vision."*
*"I courageously shine my light on the world, awakening and empowering living visions everywhere and giving all that I am toward their manifestation."*

11      **Entirety, Perfection of Being**, representing the perfection of all ten bodies.
*"I am Divine."*
*"I express divine perfection in my every thought, word and deed as I remember the truth of who I am."*

Some of these bodies, or aspects of our being, affect us specifically in certain areas of our life. We will be looking at:

      Outer Harmony and Peace
      Inner Peace
      Past Life Accomplishments
      Spiritual Path
      God's Gift To Us

It will be valuable to use the sample affirmation or to create your own to apply to the appropriate spiritual body for each specific area we explore.

Robert Waldon, ND, PhD

## OUTER HARMONY

This represents what you need to do or how you need to be to experience peace and harmony with the world around you. It is calculated by taking the number of the birth month (December becoming 3, since there is no number 12 here).

1      The **Soul** - You must learn to overcome your normal tendency to approach life analytically and come from your heart in whatever you do, not your head.
*"I am perfectly led by my heart."*
*"I totally trust and follow the guidance of my heart in all that I think, say and do."*

2      The **Negative Mind** - The negative mind calculates danger and helps you overcome any potential liabilities in connecting blindly to everyone. You need to constantly be in the company of quality people - the company of the Holy.
*"My devotion to God is all."*
*"I am devoted only to the Spirit of Love in each relationship, letting all other fears, needs and dependencies drop away."*

3      The **Positive Mind** - You must be positive in all your worldly interactions. You must see the harmony and the goodness in all things.
*"I see good and know it."*
*"I see the good in all people and events, opening me to unlimited opportunities and the experience of abundance for All."*

4      The **Neutral Mind** - You must be a good listener and allow your neutral mind to choose from the wants and avoidances, hopes and fears, positive and negative presented to you, deciding only to do that which is for the highest good.
*"I serve only the truest call."*
*"I set aside all fears and desires coming from myself and others and respond only to support the highest and best for all concerned."*

5      The **Physical Body** - You must exercise your willpower to achieve appropriate balance in your life. You may need to make apparent sacrifices which are for your own highest good.
*"I live the lessons I would teach."*
*"I learn from every life experience, choosing only for my highest good and teaching others by my living example of truth and integrity."*

6  The **Third Eye** - You must be consistent, follow through and keep your commitments to yourself. Be single focused with one-pointed concentration on whatever you do. Recognize and develop in yourself the power of your word (the ability to live up to or create precisely what you speak).

*"My focus is my power."*

*"I experience the manifested power of my every thought and word as my natural focus creates a concentration of Spirit-filled energy."*

7  The **Aura** - You must feel self-confident, extending yourself into any situation so that existing negativity is transformed (brought into the light) and won't penetrate you. Uplift any and all circumstances.

*"I am inspired as I inspire."*

*"My presence alone is a blessing to all, bringing inspiration, peace and enlightenment."*

8  **Prana** - Long range planning is important for you to be able to see the steps to be taken from where you are to where you want to be. You need to hold your highest vision, seeing the more infinite picture always. Follow through on your plans using the energy of prana.

*"In my love is all healed."*

*"I am the breath of God, bringing life and wholeness to all with the purity of my loving energy."*

9  The **Subtle Body** - You must master something (doesn't matter what) as a symbol of your mastery in the world. Repetition of something is beneficial to achieve mastery and to remember. Work out potential problems on the subtle level so all relationships work smoothly. Be graceful and innocently naive.

*"I am calm, knowing mastery of Self."*

*"I am peaceful, gentle and calm, knowing that strength and protection are found within mastery of the Self."*

10  The **Radiant Body** - Whatever you do, you must give it your all. There must be radiance in you involvement.

*"I hold to my true vision."*

*"I courageously shine my light on the world, awakening and empowering living visions everywhere and giving all that I am toward their manifestation."*

11  **Entirety, Perfection of Being** - This is mastery of the physical realm. You must hold the highest opinion of yourself as elegant, royal, divine and give yourself only the best. Be your full God-Self.

*"I am Divine."*

*"I express divine perfection in my every thought, word and deed as I remember the truth of who I am."*

## INNER PEACE

This represents what your Soul needs for inner peace and is the area that can give you the most trouble. It represents the internal process of how you deal with yourself. If you work at this and master it, then under stress you will be able to automatically communicate with your soul. The feeling of abandonment is a major obstacle to peace. Mastery here teaches that Soul is your constant companion and friend. This aspect is calculated by taking the number of the birth day.

1      The **Soul** - You must come from your heart and totally trust your heart.
       *"I am perfectly led by my heart."*
       *"I totally trust and follow the guidance of my heart in all that I think, say and do."*

2      The **Negative Mind** - You must bring all longings to a point of neutrality (not neediness). Your connection to God out weighs all other relationships to people.
       *"My devotion to God is all."*
       *"I am devoted only to the Spirit of Love in each relationship, letting all other fears, needs and dependencies drop away."*

3      The **Positive Mind** - You must see yourself as being part of God, as a Spiritual being.
       *"I see good and know it."*
       *"I see the good in all people and events, opening me to unlimited opportunities and the experience of abundance for All."*

4      The **Neutral Mind** - You must be very decisive. This is most easily done by listening only to, and totally trusting, your inner voice (it's easy to act quickly when no choices need be made).
       *"I serve only the truest call."*
       *"I set aside all fears and desires coming from myself and others and respond only to support the highest and best for all concerned."*

5      The **Physical Body** - You must seek for balance. Have the ability to forego external pleasures for inner peace.
       *"I live the lessons I would teach."*
       *"I learn from every life experience, choosing only for my highest good and teaching others by my living example of truth and integrity."*

6      The **Third Eye** - You must keep your center, your sense of self, when under stress. Focus on who you are.
*"My focus is my power."*
*"I experience the manifested power of my every thought and word as my natural focus creates a concentration of Spirit-filled energy."*

7      The **Aura** - Allow the expression of Spirit in you and through you and have it uplift your own soul.
*"I am inspired as I inspire."*
*"My presence alone is a blessing to all, bringing inspiration, peace and enlightenment."*

8      **Prana** - Be fearless. See the expansiveness and power in your relationship with God. See yourself as Infinite.
*"In my love is all healed."*
*"I am the breath of God, bringing life and wholeness to all with the purity of my loving energy."*

9      The **Subtle Body** - Be gentle with yourself. Give yourself more time and space to master things you are doing.
*"I am calm, knowing mastery of Self."*
*"I am peaceful, gentle and calm, knowing that strength and protection are found within mastery of the Self."*

10      The **Radiant Body** - No matter what you are doing, give it your all and you will be at peace.
*"I hold to my true vision."*
*"I courageously shine my light on the world, awakening and empowering living visions everywhere and giving all that I am toward their manifestation."*

11      **Entirety, Perfection of Being** - Allow God to run your life. Know He is the master.
*"I am Divine."*
*"I express divine perfection in my every thought, word and deed as I remember the truth of who I am."*

## PAST LIFE ACCOMPLISHMENTS

This aspect represents the Spiritual body that you have worked on for many lifetimes.  It is usually a part of yourself that works very well for you. It is something you can rely on and use to help you.  It is how other people see you or how you come across to others.  It is calculated as the number of the birth year.

1      The **Soul** - You are seen as very creative.
*"I am perfectly led by my heart."*
*"I totally trust and follow the guidance of my heart in all that I think, say and do."*

2      The **Negative Mind** - You are easy to talk to, seen as a friend.  You have the ability to connect with anyone and are good with relationships.
*"My devotion to God is all."*
*"I am devoted only to the Spirit of Love in each relationship, letting all other fears, needs and dependencies drop away."*

3      The **Positive Mind** - People see you as cheerful and always having a positive input.
*"I see good and know it."*
*"I see the good in all people and events, opening me to unlimited opportunities and the experience of abundance for All."*

4      The **Neutral Mind** - You are a neutral advisor and very helpful.
*"I serve only the truest call."*
*"I set aside all fears and desires coming from myself and others and respond only to support the highest and best for all concerned."*

5      The **Physical Body** - Because of your ability to set yourself aside, you are seen as the personification of God.
*"I live the lessons I would teach."*
*"I learn from every life experience, choosing only for my highest good and teaching others by my living example of truth and integrity."*

6      The **Third Eye** - You are seen as focused, one-pointed, prayerful and meditative.
*"My focus is my power."*
*"I experience the manifested power of my every thought and word as my natural focus creates a concentration of Spirit-filled energy."*

7　　　The **Aura** - Others value your uplifting and elevating presence.
*"I am inspired as I inspire."*
*"My presence alone is a blessing to all, bringing inspiration, peace and enlightenment."*

8　　　**Prana** - You are seen as fearless with the ability to always carry through.
*"In my love is all healed."*
*"I am the breath of God, bringing life and wholeness to all with the purity of my loving energy."*

9　　　The **Subtle Body** - You are seen as masterful, learning things very quickly.
*"I am calm, knowing mastery of Self."*
*"I am peaceful, gentle and calm, knowing that strength and protection are found within mastery of the Self."*

10　　The **Radiant Body** - Others see your radiance and are inspired with the energy with which you do things.
*"I hold to my true vision."*
*"I courageously shine my light on the world, awakening and empowering living visions everywhere and giving all that I am toward their manifestation."*

11　　**Entirety, Perfection of Being** - You are someone who constantly reminds people of God, in how you are and what you say.
*"I am Divine."*
*"I express divine perfection in my every thought, word and deed as I remember the truth of who I am."*

## SPIRITUAL PATH

This is what you are here to do in this life to achieve a sense of fulfillment, to see yourself as Divine. When you lose your fear, you become divine. When you feel divine you are fulfilled. When you master the Spiritual Path, your divinity begins to radiate. This aspect is not so much connected with what you actually do in this lifetime as it is related to how you do what you do. It is calculated as the sum of the month, day and year of birth.

1       The **Soul** - You have to be very creative in whatever you do in order to be fulfilled.
        *"I am perfectly led by my heart."*
        *"I totally trust and follow the guidance of my heart in all that I think, say and do."*

2       The **Negative Mind** - Devotion. You must show your deep connection, obedience and dedication to God.
        *"My devotion to God is all."*
        *"I am devoted only to the Spirit of Love in each relationship, letting all other fears, needs and dependencies drop away."*

3       The **Positive Mind** - You must pursue your humanitarian ideals, expressing your concern for everyone and desire for equality for all.
        *"I see good and know it."*
        *"I see the good in all people and events, opening me to unlimited opportunities and the experience of abundance for All."*

4       The **Neutral Mind** - You must express yourself in service through choosing for the highest good (not necessarily what people say they want or are trying to avoid).
        *"I serve only the truest call."*
        *"I set aside all fears and desires coming from myself and others and respond only to support the highest and best for all concerned."*

5       The **Physical Body** - You are a teacher by example. You must live your example and be the personification of what you teach.
        *"I live the lessons I would teach."*
        *"I learn from every life experience, choosing only for my highest good and teaching others by my living example of truth and integrity."*

6   The **Third Eye** - Meditation and concentration in whatever you do. Be a holy person, a representative of God.
*"My focus is my power."*
*"I experience the manifested power of my every thought and word as my natural focus creates a concentration of Spirit-filled energy."*


7   The **Aura** - You must give inspiration, help people feel hope and uplift humanity.
*"I am inspired as I inspire."*
*"My presence alone is a blessing to all, bringing inspiration, peace and enlightenment."*

8   **Prana** - You are a healer, the Breath of God. Use breath, music, singing, etc. to heal. You have the purity and energy to follow God.
*"In my love is all healed."*
*"I am the breath of God, bringing life and wholeness to all with the purity of my loving energy."*

9   The **Subtle Body** - You must be masterful and exhibit total calm in whatever you do.
*"I am calm, knowing mastery of Self."*
*"I am peaceful, gentle and calm, knowing that strength and protection are found within mastery of the Self."*

10   The **Radiant Body** - Yours is the path of the visionary, of royal courage and high energy. You will stand out in whatever you do.
*"I hold to my true vision."*
*"I courageously shine my light on the world, awakening and empowering living visions everywhere and giving all that I am toward their manifestation."*

11   **Entirety, Perfection of Being** - You must become a constant reminder of God to other people. You can expand them to a recognition of their Infinity.
*"I am Divine."*
*"I express divine perfection in my every thought, word and deed as I remember the truth of who I am."*

## GOD'S GIFT

This represents the Spiritual body which is your gift from God in this lifetime. It is not something you need to work on or develop. It is something that works well for you, something you can rely on, your basis for strength. As long as you accept your gift, you have the ability to tune in to your Soul. If you experience this gift not working for you in your life, consciously claim the gift and then know that it is yours in that moment. This aspect is calculated as the sum of the last 2 digits from the birth year.

1       The **Soul** - You are super-creative with the ability to always come from the heart as long as you are on your spiritual path.
        *"I am perfectly led by my heart."*
        *"I totally trust and follow the guidance of my heart in all that I think, say and do."*

2       The **Negative Mind** - You have the ability to connect to anyone and make everyone feel relaxed.
        *"My devotion to God is all."*
        *"I am devoted only to the Spirit of Love in each relationship, letting all other fears, needs and dependencies drop away."*

3       The **Positive Mind** - You have a cheerful attitude and always have a positive word or thought to share.
        *"I see good and know it."*
        *"I see the good in all people and events, opening me to unlimited opportunities and the experience of abundance for All."*

4       The **Neutral Mind** - You have a "yogic" mind, neutral, humble and loving service.
        *"I serve only the truest call."*
        *"I set aside all fears and desires coming from myself and others and respond only to support the highest and best for all concerned."*

5       The **Physical Body** - You have the ability to teach by example, to model in your day to day living what you would have others learn.
        *"I live the lessons I would teach."*
        *"I learn from every life experience, choosing only for my highest good and teaching others by my living example of truth and integrity."*

6       The **Third Eye** - You can be totally focused and one-pointed about everything you do, to bring the power of your concentration into successful action and accomplishment.
*"My focus is my power."*
*"I experience the manifested power of my every thought and word as my natural focus creates a concentration of Spirit-filled energy."*

7       The **Aura** - You have the ability to uplift any situation and bring Spirit into it.
*"I am inspired as I inspire."*
*"My presence alone is a blessing to all, bringing inspiration, peace and enlightenment."*

8       **Prana** - You are fearless, knowing your relationship with God.
*"In my love is all healed."*
*"I am the breath of God, bringing life and wholeness to all with the purity of my loving energy."*

9       The **Subtle Body** - You can master situations quickly and understand the subtleties involved.
*"I am calm, knowing mastery of Self."*
*"I am peaceful, gentle and calm, knowing that strength and protection are found within mastery of the Self."*

10      The **Radiant Body** - Whatever you apply yourself to radiates.
*"I hold to my true vision."*
*"I courageously shine my light on the world, awakening and empowering living visions everywhere and giving all that I am toward their manifestation."*

11      **Entirety, Perfection of Being** - You are able to express the energy of any aspect of your being when needed, to be and express any aspect of God.
*"I am Divine."*
*"I express divine perfection in my every thought, word and deed as I remember the truth of who I am."*

# CURRENT SOUL CONNECTIONS

None of us come together "by accident". We all have a specific teaching/ learning to share in every relationship. Some joinings have added significance, representing a connection that is to be of greater importance or duration.

These Current Soul Connections can be best understood by examining the symbols of the Ten Spiritual Bodies as they apply to yourself (as you saw in the previous section) and to another or others with whom you are in relationship. (You can refer to the previous section and to the Calculations section to arrive at aspects for others.)

Whenever the same Spiritual Body occurs in the same aspect of your life and the life of another (i.e. Outer Harmony, Inner Peace, Past Life Accomplishment, Spiritual Path or Gift), the two of you share an important soul connection in this lifetime. This represents an area where you will have greater potential understanding, joining and support for each other. Because the aspect is shared, you will be able to work together or to inspire each other in your individual expression.

**For Example:**

|          | Outer Harmony | Inner Peace | Past Accomp. | Spiritual Path | God's Gift |
|----------|------|------|------|------|------|
| Me       | 5 | 9 | 4  | 9 | 3 |
| Daughter | 5 | 7 | 10 | 4 | 9 |

My daughter and I have the fifth Spiritual Body (physical body, teacher by example) in the aspect of Outer Harmony. We are both very aware of how to recognize and support what is needed for each other to achieve harmony with our outer worlds. Also, being the body of teaching by example, the way we conduct our individual lives is a reminder/teaching for the other.

In addition to just seeing the areas of connection, you can refer back to the specific expression of the Spiritual Body in that aspect of your life to give you greater insight into the potential of the relationship.

When no aspects are shared, it just means that your coming together is not focused on a particular area.

## SPIRITUAL CHALLENGES

Spiritual Challenges are neither "good" nor "bad", they are merely challenges. They are areas of extra energy in the relationship and serve as ways we can wake each other up and inspire each other to our full potential. What shows up here are the "patterns" of challenge, the specific area in which we have been called together to assist each other in getting on and staying on purpose.

Specific Spiritual Challenges are represented in relationships where the same Spiritual Body occurs in **different** aspects of your life and the life of another with whom you are in relationship. When both of you are living your lives (or at least that aspect of your expression) "on purpose", there will be synergy and inspiration. When one is living "off purpose", somehow withholding the full, free expression of that aspect of their life, that person can be uplifted by the other. Of course, the more on purpose individual can choose to join the other in diminished expression, which does neither of them much good. Therein lies the challenge. It's up to the most conscious being in any relationship, at any given moment, to continue to fully express the truth of who they are. It is the only way to stay awake and to reawaken others.

Using my daughter and I as in the previous example:

|  | Outer Harmony | Inner Peace | Past Accomp. | Spiritual Path | God's Gift |
|---|---|---|---|---|---|
| Me | 5 | 9 | 4 | 9 | 3 |
| Daughter | 5 | 7 | 10 | 4 | 9 |

There are two areas of Spiritual Challenge. The first affects both my Inner Peace and my Spiritual Path, represented by the ninth Spiritual Body (subtle body, mastery and calm). This is my daughter's Gift in that she can quickly and easily master any situation and see the subtleties in it. In her expression of her gift, I am reminded/inspired regarding how I need to be for Inner Peace and to fully express on my Spiritual Path. Also, as I experience Inner Peace and am on purpose in life, she is reminded of her Gift, which she can claim and use at any time.

The other area of challenge is my aspect of Past Life Accomplishment and her Spiritual Path, both represented by the fourth Spiritual Body (neutral mind, service). Because I am seen as a neutral advisor and very serviceful, she can be inspired by my example to serve others on her Spiritual Path by choosing for the highest good in every circumstance. Conversely, as I experience her being on purpose in life, I am reminded of a very valuable aspect of myself that I can call on at any time.

Again, looking at the specific expression of each body in the affected aspects may provide greater insight into harmonious and inspiring relationships.

**Robert Waldon, ND, PhD**

## SPIRITUAL BODIES

1 Soul - creativity, humility
2 Negative Mind - longing to belong, devotion
3 Positive Mind - equality
4 Neutral Mind - service
5 Physical Body - teacher by example
6 Third Eye - one pointed concentration
7 Aura - mercy, uplifting
8 Prana - purity, healing
9 Subtle Body - calmness, mastery
10 Radiant Body - visionary, royal courage
11 Entirety, Perfection of Being - the infinite

## CURRENT SOUL CONNECTIONS

| Name | Outer Harmony | Inner Peace | Past Accomp. | Spiritual Path | God's Gift |
|---|---|---|---|---|---|

## SPIRITUAL CHALLENGES

| Name | Outer Harmony | Inner Peace | Past Accomp. | Spiritual Path | God's Gift |
|---|---|---|---|---|---|

94

# RELATIONSHIP TO THE WORLD

Robert Waldon, ND, PhD

# RELATIONSHIP TO THE WORLD

There are four primary aspects of your world to which you relate in different ways: Physical, Emotional, Mental and Creative. It is important to understand how you relate to each aspect of your world so that you do not judge yourself, criticize yourself or misunderstand who you are. In non-judgmental understanding, you are able to see the strengths in the way you are and become more powerful and more obvious in the display of your individual gifts, your unique contribution to the overall plan.

Below is an overview of some characteristics of each way of being. You can refer back to this for expansion of your own relationship to each aspect of your world as described in the following sections. Astrological correlations are included for added clarity.

## #1  MANIFESTOR

Symbolized by the sign of Taurus and expressed as **"I Have"**.

Possessions, practicality, purposeful determination and power, mastery over the physical, efficient in practical matters, aggregation, building, endurance, gathering, collecting, consolidation, strong sense of values, sense of self-worth, wants tangible results, sensory involvement.

Ruled by Venus (social, romantic and artistic expression, formulation of values)
Earth Sign (practicality, ability to accumulate and manage money and material resources)
Fixed Sign (future or goal oriented, achieves results from persistence, perseverance and determination)

## #2  SENSITIVE

Symbolized by the sign of Cancer and expressed as **"I Feel"**.

Domesticity, sensitivity, tenacity, intuition, emotional sensitivity, highly developed protective and defensive instincts, need for security, cooperative, patient, understanding, flexible, adaptable, need to establish boundaries, nurturing.

Ruled by the Moon (feelings, subconscious mind, emotional patterns, spontaneous response)
Water Sign (emotions and feelings, sensitivity and intuition, focused on home and family)
Cardinal Sign (present moment, ability to act directly and decisively on present circumstances)

96

## #3  WILLFUL EXPRESSER

Symbolized by the sign of Leo and expressed as **"I Will"**

Vitality, authority, power, Royalty, generosity and nobility, dramatic, enthusiastic, inspirational, practical, philosophical, spiritual, stamina, durable, creative self-expression.

Ruled by the Sun (power, life force, brilliance, exuberance, self-identity, purpose)
Fire Sign (leadership, central figure, managerial ability)
Fixed Sign (future, goal oriented, achieves results from persistence, perseverance and determination)

## #4  HARMONIZER

Symbolized by the sign of Libra and expressed as **"I Serve"**.

Harmony, companionship, balance, strong sense of justice and fair play, peace maker, willing to fight for what's right, loving, romantic, affectionate, cooperative, learning through interaction.

Ruled by Venus (social, romantic and artistic expression, formulation of values)
Air Sign (social & mental/intellectual, ability to weigh and balance)
Cardinal Sign (present moment, ability to act directly and decisively on present circumstances)

## #5  CREATOR

Symbolized by the sign of Aries and expressed as **"I Am"**.

Initiative, activity, enterprise, constructive freedom, new beginnings, enthusiasm, direct in expression, impulsive doer, competitive, great will power and spiritual self-confidence, self-motivated, pioneer, trying new experiences.

Ruled by Mars (expression, action, assertiveness, bold determination)
Fire Sign (leadership, decisiveness, spearheading new endeavors)
Cardinal Sign (present moment, ability to act directly and decisively on present circumstances)

## #6  COMMUNICATOR

Symbolized by the sign of Gemini and expressed as **"I Think"**.

Mentality, versatility, nonconformist, inventive, imaginative, likes variety, speech and communication, need good education, changeable, exacting, analytical, childlike curiosity.

Ruled by Mercury (thinking and communication, rational mind)
Air Sign (social and mental/intellectual, acquire, utilize and communicate factual information)
Mutable Sign (past, adaptable, flexible, ingenious, builds skills from previous experience)

## #7  EXPLORER

Symbolized by the sign of Sagittarius and expressed as **"I See"**.

Aspiration, love of freedom, travel & exploration, ability to see future by understanding current trends, honest, straightforward, idealistic, energetic, outgoing, goals achieved through power of positive thinking, confident, motivational.

Ruled by Jupiter (religion & philosophy, expansiveness, generous, confident, optimistic)
Fire Sign (leadership, spiritual/philosophic leader)
Mutable Sign (past, adaptable, flexible, ingenious, builds skills from previous experience)

## #8  ORGANIZER

Symbolized by the sign of Capricorn and expressed as **"I Use"**.

Ambition, conservatism, conscientiousness, organization, realistic, steady, sure-footed, intuitive, loves law and order, capacity for hard work, goal oriented, serious, practical wisdom, "old when young and young when old".

Ruled by Saturn (responsibility, maturity, discipline, work & career, patient, disciplined, responsible, reliable, internal authority)
Earth Sign (practicality, organize and manage large enterprises)
Cardinal Sign (present moment, ability to act directly and decisively on present circumstances)

## #9  HUMANITARIAN

Symbolized by the sign of Virgo and expressed as **"I Analyze"**.

Discrimination, methodical, service through seeing how everything goes together, perfectionist, seeks knowledge to control matter, wisdom from experience, systematic, attention to detail.

Ruled by Mercury (thinking and communication, rational mind)
Also associated with the Asteroid Belt (regeneration, bringing together, reunion, putting together the puzzle)
Earth Sign (practicality, intelligence and skill in constructing material objects, maintaining the body)
Mutable Sign (past, adaptable, flexible, ingenious, builds skills from previous experience)

## #11  IDEALIST

Symbolized by the sign of Pisces and expressed as **"I Believe"**.

Compassion, universality, renunciation, inspirational, visionary, imaginative, responsive to thoughts and feelings of others, duality of emotions, idealistic, abstract, perceptive, accepting of everyone and everything.

Ruled by Neptune (health & growth of society, personal psychological health relative to others, visualization, imagination, connection to God, creativity)
Water Sign (emotions & feelings, sensitivity & intuition, mystical, telepathic)
Mutable Sign (past, adaptable, flexible, ingenious, builds skills from previous experience)

## #22  BUILDER OF NEW WORLDS

Symbolized by the sign of Aquarius and expressed as **"I Know"**.

Humanitarian, independent, originality, nonconformist, eccentric, powerful, friendship and groups, determined, stubborn, best work is for some ideal or for benefit of mankind, willing to fight the system, freedom from old established ways of doing things.

Ruled by Uranus (beyond personality, group creative expression, unexpected changes and opportunities, imaginative, inventive, impulsive)
Air Sign (social & mental/intellectual, intuitive grasp of universal principles, concern for universal well-being)
Fixed Sign (future, goal oriented, achieves results from persistence, perseverance and determination)

## #33 **TRANSFORMER**

Symbolized by the sign of Scorpio and expressed as **"I Transform"**.

Regeneration, resourceful, secrecy, transmutation, rebirth, fundamental transformation on all levels, power, will, intense emotional desires, investigate and discover underlying causes, not limited by past or convention, transformation through merging, healing, passion, intensity.

Ruled by Pluto (dramatic & permanent transformation and change, death/rebirth, transforming personal consciousness, universal sense of self)
Water Sign (emotions & feelings, sensitivity & intuition)
Fixed Sign (future, goal oriented, achieves results from persistence, perseverance and determination)

## RELATION TO PHYSICAL

This includes your relationship with your body and the bodies of others, your things & possessions, the physical form of the earth and the objects in, on and around it, your home/physical living space, your money, etc., etc..

This aspect is calculated by taking the number of your birth month as a number from 1 through 9 and the master number 11 (Oct. = 1 and Dec. = 3).

1   Manifestor - "I Have"
> Need for material comfort, things form part of the identity of the self, ownership and possession, sensory involvement, carry through, leadership.
> *"I have what I choose."*
> *"My strong sense of purpose and personal values powerfully create the manifestation of my desires."*

2   Sensitive - "I Feel"
> Sensory awareness, sensations felt on a physical level, nurturing environment, protective of physical world, adaptable, attention to detail.
> *"I feel the truth in my relationships."*
> *"My intuition, sensitivity and understanding guide me in the perfect nurturing expression in each moment for myself and others."*

3   Willful Expresser - "I Will"
> Willing or commanding things to be the way you want them to be, things of highest quality, generous, self-expressive, artistic, optimistic.
> *"I will and it is so."*
> *"My vitality, enthusiasm and full expression create the world I choose."*

4   Harmonizer - "I Serve"
> Want to have things work for and serve everyone, make everyone happy, want the world a certain way, beauty, grace, design, carries out plans, systematic and orderly, organizer, leader.
> *"I serve the truth."*
> *"My decisive, powerful action serves all in the achievement of our highest goals."*

5   Creator - "I Am"
> Creating a creative environment, learns from life experiences with the physical world, vitality, lots of activity.
> *"I am as I create."*
> *"I am the perfect creation, alive in the process of becoming and actively expressing myself in my world."*

6    Communicator - "I Think"

Bringing ideas into physical expression (esp. writing), primary need to feel connected to physical environment, likes order, beauty and harmony, sensitive to environmental disruption, responsible, serves others.

*"My ideas inspire all."*

*"My powerful mind and inventive imagination expand myself and my world as they are shared."*

7    Explorer - "I See"

Travel, seeing higher meaning to worldly aspects, physical activity and competition, demands perfection (from self and others), discrimination, selective, wants the best.

*"I open to new vistas."*

*"I am open and free, ready to experience all the world has to offer and more."*

8    Organizer - "I Use"

Physical world is a tool or means to an end, make the best use of whatever is available, organization of resources, accomplishment, material comfort and satisfaction.

*"I use all for its highest good."*

*"My practicality and sense of organization empower excellent accomplishment in my world."*

9    Humanitarian - "I Analyze"

Uses knowledge to control matter, things seen as valuable only as they serve higher purposes, sensual, orderly and perfect, ability to care for and maintain what they have.

*"I analyze and see our way to Oneness."*

*"My clear vision of the whole brings all pieces of my world into harmonious and right relationship."*

11   Idealist - "I Believe"

Sees the good in the way things are, may self-sacrifice for the good of others.

*"I believe the true and good."*

*"I hold true to my highest visions and see the perfection in all creation."*

# RELATION TO EMOTIONS

This includes your full range of feelings and those of others and how you express/experience them. This aspect is calculated as the day of birth expressed as a number from 1 through 9 and the master numbers 11 and 22.

1 Manifestor - "I Have"
>Wants pleasure and enjoyment, desire for new and different, determination to keep own feelings private, allows others to "own" their own feelings, stands on convictions and beliefs.
>*"I have what I choose."*
>*"My strong sense of purpose and personal values powerfully create the manifestation of my desires."*

2 Sensitive - "I Feel"
>Need emotional security (can nurture others only when self is secure), protective of feelings, want full experience of feelings, need to teach and learn it is healthy and safe to fully emote, patient and diplomatic, sensitive to feelings.
>*"I feel the truth in my relationships."*
>*"My intuition, sensitivity and understanding guide me in the perfect nurturing expression in each moment for myself and others."*

3 Willful Expresser - "I Will"
>Dramatic, powerful, want to have fun, love of life comes from following heart, responsive, expressive, loving.
>*"I will and it is so."*
>*"My vitality, enthusiasm and full expression create the world I choose."*

4 Harmonizer - "I Serve"
>Peace maker (inner & outer), want flowing relationships without problems, serious, conscientious, stable, faithful.
>*"I serve the truth."*
>*"My decisive, powerful action serves all in the achievement of our highest goals."*

5 Creator - "I Am"
>Emotions expressed through creative endeavors, need to follow emotional responses, enthusiastic, strong feelings, need variety in emotional self-expression.
>*"I am as I create."*
>*"I am the perfect creation, alive in the process of becoming and actively expressing myself in my world."*

6   Communicator - "I Think"
>   Thinking about feelings, factual about emotions, feels deeply, sensitive
>   to others, desires affection.
>   *"My ideas inspire all."*
>   *"My powerful mind and inventive imagination expand myself and my world as they
>   are shared."*

7   Explorer - "I See"
>   Wants to see and explore all emotions of self and others and to expand
>   out of emotional limits, introspective, sometimes distant, rational or
>   logical approach.
>   *"I open to new vistas."*
>   *"I am open and free, ready to experience all the world has to offer and more."*

8   Organizer - "I Use"
>   Feelings only valued when useful, overcautious in expression, self-
>   reliant, disciplined emotions, non-sentimental.
>   *"I use all for its highest good."*
>   *"My practicality and sense of organization empower excellent accomplishment in my
>   world."*

9   Humanitarian - "I Analyze"
>   Analysis of emotions to see how they serve the highest good, wants to
>   perfect self through examining and refining responses, intense
>   emotions, compassionate and sensitive to needs and feelings of others.
>   *"I analyze and see our way to Oneness."*
>   *"My clear vision of the whole brings all pieces of my world into harmonious and
>   right relationship."*

11  Idealist - "I Believe"
>   Need to feel their intense emotions, compassion for others, feel better
>   when others do.
>   *"I believe the true and good."*
>   *"I hold true to my highest visions and see the perfection in all creation."*

22  Builder of New Worlds - "I Know"
>   Passion for universal well-being, need for freedom, sees personal
>   feelings unimportant compared to problems of the world.
>   *"I know and all is manifest."*
>   *"I create my ideal world for all through the strength and clarity of my vision and the
>   power which flows through me for its manifestation."*

# RELATION TO MENTAL

This includes thoughts, thought processes, beliefs, ideas belonging to yourself and others, etc.. This aspect is calculated as the year of birth expressed as a number from 1 through 9 and the master numbers of 11, 22 and 33.

1   Manifestor - "I Have"

Personal ownership of ideas, have a "mind of your own", may be stubborn and inflexible, original thinker, creative mind.
*"I have what I choose."*
*"My strong sense of purpose and personal values powerfully create the manifestation of my desires."*

2   Sensitive - "I Feel"

Very intuitive, protective & defensive about ideas and careful who they are shared with, gathers facts and information, detail-oriented thought process.
*"I feel the truth in my relationships."*
*"My intuition, sensitivity and understanding guide me in the perfect nurturing expression in each moment for myself and others."*

3   Willful Expresser - "I Will"

Inspiring and practical ideas, want them shared and noticed by others, creative, imaginative, quick mind.
*"I will and it is so."*
*"My vitality, enthusiasm and full expression create the world I choose."*

4   Harmonizer - "I Serve"

Willing to fight for ideas, create mental images of how things should be, ideas foster cooperation, fair play and justice, takes charge, organized thought, practical.
*"I serve the truth."*
*"My decisive, powerful action serves all in the achievement of our highest goals."*

5   Creator - "I Am"

Lots of original ideas, need to flow & not get stuck in any, no predetermined, preconceived ideas, quick, curious, investigative, seeks knowledge, shares/teaches wisdom.
*"I am as I create."*
*"I am the perfect creation, alive in the process of becoming and actively expressing myself in my world."*

6   Communicator - "I Think"
    Knowing and communicating that knowing, search for mental
    stimulation, may engage in "mental gymnastics", concentration/focus,
    systematic, high ideals.
    *"My ideas inspire all."*
    *"My powerful mind and inventive imagination expand myself and my world as they
    are shared."*

7   Explorer - "I See"
    Spiritual ideas, seeking higher meaning, expanding the boundaries of
    thought, search for higher truth, may hold some thoughts private,
    analytical.
    *"I open to new vistas."*
    *"I am open and free, ready to experience all the world has to offer and more."*

8   Organizer - "I Use"
    Practical, organized ideas, know when, where and how they fit, handle
    large projects well, ability to weigh and balance, well disciplined mind.
    *"I use all for its highest good."*
    *"My practicality and sense of organization empower excellent accomplishment in my
    world."*

9   Humanitarian - "I Analyze"
    Seeing how things fit together, how to improve things and make them
    more efficient to serve everyone, abstract thought, visionary, ideas for
    reunion of all humanity in love.
    *"I analyze and see our way to Oneness."*
    *"My clear vision of the whole brings all pieces of my world into harmonious and
    right relationship."*

11  Idealist - "I Believe"
    Need to understand and unify experiences, idealistic, universal, active
    imagination.
    *"I believe the true and good."*
    *"I hold true to my highest visions and see the perfection in all creation."*

22  Builder of New Worlds - "I Know"
    New ideas, concepts and values for the New Age, abstract thinking for
    the benefit of mankind.
    *"I know and all is manifest."*
    *"I create my ideal world for all through the strength and clarity of my vision and the
    power which flows through me for its manifestation."*

33  Transformer - "I Desire"

Not too concerned with conventional wisdom, investigate, discover and transform underlying causes.

*"I transform my world with conscious intention."*

*"I create change through the rebirth of my personal consciousness and the transformation of my world to its highest expression."*

## RELATION TO SPIRITUAL CREATIVITY

This includes your own personal creativity, but more importantly, your creative, spiritual expression in the world. This involves how and for what purposes you interact with others and it relates specifically to your "doingness" in this world, your work, job, career, etc. This aspect is calculated as the total of the month, day and year of birth expressed as a number from 1 through 9 and the master numbers 11, 22 and 33.

1   Manifestor - "I Have"
>    Mastery over physical things; consciousness, growth and spirituality found through experiences in the material world, power of concentration, visualization and manifestation.
>    *"I have what I choose."*
>    *"My strong sense of purpose and personal values powerfully create the manifestation of my desires."*

2   Sensitive - "I Feel"
>    Create a safe place for self and family, nurturing and sense of belonging in the world for self and others, receptive to inner revelation and intuition.
>    *"I feel the truth in my relationships."*
>    *"My intuition, sensitivity and understanding guide me in the perfect nurturing expression in each moment for myself and others."*

3   Willful Expresser - "I Will"
>    Authority, central figure, opening new expressions of self and others, open channel for inspiration, intuitive, inspirational.
>    *"I will and it is so."*
>    *"My vitality, enthusiasm and full expression create the world I choose."*

4   Harmonizer - "I Serve"
>    Leader, bring people to peace and harmony, create support systems, manifestor of dreams and visions, creates order, practicality for the highest good, service.
>    *"I serve the truth."*
>    *"My decisive, powerful action serves all in the achievement of our highest goals."*

5   Creator - "I Am"
> Inspiring, spiritual, creative, new forms/ways, sense of self derives from creative work, self-motivated, intuitive, creates variety and change, willingness to be different.
> *"I am as I create."*
> *"I am the perfect creation, alive in the process of becoming and actively expressing myself in my world."*

6   Communicator - "I Think"
> Creating from thoughts and teaching facts, opening to new avenues of communication, intuitive, sixth sense.
> *"My ideas inspire all."*
> *"My powerful mind and inventive imagination expand myself and my world as they are shared."*

7   Explorer - "I See"
> Spiritual/philosophical leader & explorer, awareness of potential, focus on large picture, expands people's world view, interest in discovering highest truths.
> *"I open to new vistas."*
> *"I am open and free, ready to experience all the world has to offer and more."*

8   Organizer - "I Use"
> Manager, putting things and people to best use, philosophies, morals and laws brought to form, practical results, brings spiritual truth into tangible form.
> *"I use all for its highest good."*
> *"My practicality and sense of organization empower excellent accomplishment in my world."*

9   Humanitarian - "I Analyze"
> Bringing all the pieces together for highest good, creates community, urge to refine creative expression to perfection, team player, idealistic dreams and visions manifest in selfless service.
> *"I analyze and see our way to Oneness."*
> *"My clear vision of the whole brings all pieces of my world into harmonious and right relationship."*

11   Idealist - "I Believe"
>   Integrates physical and spiritual, creates for health, growth and welfare of society.
>   *"I believe the true and good."*
>   *"I hold true to my highest visions and see the perfection in all creation."*

22   Builder of New Worlds - "I Know"
>   All creation is from highest vision  and purpose with a goal for the benefit of mankind, express personal uniqueness, draw attention to areas needing reform.
>   *"I know and all is manifest."*
>   *"I create my ideal world for all through the strength and clarity of my vision and the power which flows through me for its manifestation."*

33   Transformer - "I Desire"
>   Dramatic and permanent transformation and change, rising above perceived limitations.
>   *"I transform my world with conscious intention."*
>   *"I create change through the rebirth of my personal consciousness and the transformation of my world to its highest expression."*

## PAST SOUL CONNECTIONS

At this stage of our evolution, most of those with whom you are in current relationship have been connected with you at some time in the past. Some of these connections have a direct and specific bearing on your being together in this lifetime. It may be to re-experience some past association, to "clean up" or finish some old business, to build on previous experience, etc..

What will show up here are Past Soul Connections which have a specific purpose relative to what you are here to do in this lifetime. If no Past Soul Connections show up, it doesn't mean none exist. It merely means that your coming together in this lifetime is for present lifetime work only.

These Past Soul Connections show up in areas where you and another have the same numerological symbols in the same area of Relationship To The World. Matching numbers in the Physical area indicates a previous **blood tie** (parent/child, sibling, family). Connections in the Emotional area indicate a previous **love bond** (lovers, husband/wife, deep loving friendship). Connections in the Mental area indicate previous **cognitive connections** (teacher/student, students together, learning situations). Connections in the Creative area indicate a previous **inspirational bond** (spiritual work together, joined in a high cause, members of a religious order).

**For Example:**

| Name | Physical Creative (blood tie) (inspirational) | Emotional (love bond) | Mental (cognate) | |
|---|---|---|---|---|
| Me | 5 | 9 | 22 | 9 |
| Mother | 8 | 3 | 7 | 9 |

My mother and I share the number 9 (Humanitarian) in the Creative area. This would indicate that we had previously been joined in an inspirational cause and, looking at the nature of the number 9, it would have been for a Humanitarian goal of some kind. This is a connection we brought into this lifetime and an area where we understand each other, have inspired each other and have created the space for each other to express and pursue our work. It is an area where we have joined efforts in this lifetime at various times when it was called for.

Looking at the Past Soul Connection alone can give you a good indication of why you might feel strongly drawn to or joined with another. Looking into the full meaning of the number itself will give you greater insights into what that joining means and how to express it to the fullest.

**Robert Waldon, ND, PhD**

## WORLDLY CHALLENGES

Like Spiritual Challenges, Worldly Challenges are not good or bad. They are challenges to become, and to stay, conscious so that every relationship can be inspiring to all. We usually become aware of our Worldly Challenges by noticing what is **not** working in a relationship, where the other person gets to us, pushes our buttons or interferes with our life or full free expression. Good! That's the "wake up call". What you do with that call is up to you. You can resist it, run from it, try to change the other person (all of these, of course, being at the effect of the challenge) or you can look for the **seeds of inspiration**. Look for the ways you are off purpose which allow this to "bump" you. Use it to get back on purpose. Find the way in which the two of you **can** relate and support each other, without any sacrifice or compromise. That's the true gift.

Using the analogy of gears in a car, when you are moving down the road and shifting from second gear to third gear, there is definitely a call to "come together" in order to enhance rapid forward progress. When one or both of the gears are "out of synch" they will grind. In our relationships, we call this conflict. The solution is to move into a neutral position, get "on purpose", aligned, then come together again.

What will show up here are only those relationships where there is a "pattern" of challenge, a specific call to be together to create "on purposeness" in one or more specific areas of your life. If there is no pattern which shows up here, you can still use each relationship "bump" to consciously wake you up by noticing what area of your life was affected, where you were bumped. That is the area which is currently being called to your attention as being off purpose in some way.

**For Example:**

| Name | Physical Creative | Emotional | Mental | |
|------|------|------|------|------|
| Me | 5 | 9 | 22 | 9 |
| Brother | 9 | 8 | 5 | 22 |

My brother and I are about as different as could be and we have had lots of challenges. From the above chart you can see that the way he relates to the world Mentally (his thoughts and thought process) could (and did) interfere with how I related to my world Physically, specifically dealing with my environment (our shared room), money and our material possessions. His Physical impacted my Emotions and Creativity. My Mental and his Creative held potential for conflict, but was generally inspiring to me from the start. Obviously, all of these

112

connections had some effect on him as well. We now have a wonderful, loving and supportive relationship, one that inspires us both in almost every area of our lives.

You can pay close attention to the actual number meanings to give you clues on how to change any areas of conflict to areas of inspiration. Remember, as in the example of my brother and me, the more challenges present, the more potentially powerful and inspiring the relationship. Also remember, it is up to the most conscious being, at any given moment, to take responsibility for living his life on purpose and finding the loving, supportive way in any relationship. Your partner will gladly wake up and follow as soon as he/you see a better way. There is **never** anything to "fix" in the other person. It is **always** a call to get your own life back on purpose.

## RELATIONSHIP TO THE WORLD

1   Manifestor - "I Have"
2   Sensitive - "I Feel"
3   Willful Expresser - "I Will"
4   Harmonizer - "I Serve"
5   Creator - "I Am"
6   Communicator - "I Think"
7   Explorer - "I See"
8   Organizer - "I Use"
9   Humanitarian - "I Analyze"
11   Idealist - "I Believe"
22   Builder of New Worlds - "I Know"
33   Transformer - "I Desire"

## PAST SOUL CONNECTIONS

| | Physical Creative | Emotional | Mental |
|---|---|---|---|
| Name (inspirational) | (blood tie) | (love bond) | (cognate) |

## WORLDLY CHALLENGES

| Name | Physical Creative | Emotional | Mental |
|---|---|---|---|

# YOUR CURRENT LIFETIME

# YOUR CURRENT LIFETIME

## COLLECTIVE EXPERIENCE

Your collective experience represents the accumulated benefits of your history, your past lives, the collective wisdom which you bring from the past that shapes your mental pursuits, visions, your inspirations and aspirations in this lifetime. These are the gifts from your past that you bring to your present experience. This aspect is calculated as the sum of all the letters in your full birth name expressed as a number from 1 through 9 plus the Master Numbers 11, 22, 33, 44, 55, 66, 77, 88 and 99. (See section at the beginning of the book for calculation procedures.)

## LIFE PATH

Your life path represents your present choices for this incarnation, the new opportunities and experiences you have chosen, what you have come to accomplish at this time. It represents what you need to accomplish to experience fulfillment in this lifetime. This aspect is calculated as the total of the month, day and year of birth expressed as a number from 1 through 9 or one of the Master Numbers 11, 22, 33, 44, 55, 66, 77, 88 or 99.

## ULTIMATE LIFETIME GOAL

The ultimate goal represents your Soul's highest purpose in this lifetime. Your past gifts and your present choices both blend to manifest the realization of this, your spiritual ambition. It is a goal that will be ever more clearly realized as it unfolds from the accumulated experiences and lessons of your life. This aspect is calculated as the sum of the Collective Experience number and the Life Path number, expressed as a number from 1 through 9 or one of the Master Numbers.

## NUMEROLOGICAL DESCRIPTIONS

The following pages outline some of the basic numerical meanings as they apply to the above three aspects of your Self. You may also benefit from applying other symbolic or numerical descriptions (found in other sections of the book) which are related to your specific number as a way of gaining additional insights.

## 1   INDEPENDENCE, CREATIVITY

New ideas, creativity, starting new things, like to work alone, manifest God power on earth, seek new adventures, strong leadership, willpower, self-reliant, inspiration, mental energy, individuation, attainment from personal effort, first be independent then be a leader or creator and significant attainment follows. Leadership and independence. Success through following original ideas and personal creation.

*"I am ready to begin."*

*"I confidently and creatively express my originality as I manifest my inspiration in the world."*

## 2   COOPERATION, JOINING

Unifying duality, group and community work, diplomacy, sensitivity, balance and equilibrium, mediator, supportive, adaptable, considerate, helpful, decisions between two or more things, organizer, facilitator, power behind the throne, skill in working with others.

Cooperation and balancing apparent dualities in the world (light/dark, male/female, etc.) through sensitivity to the Divine. Peacemaker and diplomat for the benefit of all.

*"I join and know love."*

*"My sensitivity to Divine guidance leads me in the reconciliation of apparent polarities and in the joining of all in shared vision and purpose."*

## 3   JOYFUL SELF-EXPRESSION

Union of Divine and human qualities, creativity, expression, imagination, inspiration, artistic, optimistic, entertaining, enjoys luxury, joy of living, innocently naive, creative self-expression, talent with words.

Fully express all creative talents and ideas and inspire and fill others with joy and happiness.

*"I love to express my Self."*

*"My full, free self-expression is an inspiration and blessing, opening the world to the experience of greater joy and happiness."*

## 4   DISCIPLINE, SERVICE

Bringing spiritual energy into form, leadership, service, establishing systems and order, practical, builder, perseverance, responsible, hard working, overcoming and using real and apparent limitations, high standards, courage, honesty, learn advantages of order and system, see how limitations and order serve service, rewards of service, patience, dependability.

Manifest visions and dreams in material form. Bring order and system into the world to create permanence of the good. Build foundation for the New World.

*"I lead from my inner strength."*

*"I easily and powerfully manifest the highest visions in material form, in loving service for the benefit and freedom of all."*

## 5 CONSTRUCTIVE FREEDOM

Curiosity, change, vitality, unconventional, detachment, teaching/learning from interactions with life, choosing from wide variety of opportunities, intellectual, imaginative, expressive, freedom of thought and action, counselor, teacher, learn constructive use of freedom, not waste time or scatter energy, pick and choose experiences, discard what doesn't work.

Be independent and free to explore all life has to offer. Constantly teach and learn by getting all possible meaning from every life experience and opening new possibilities for progress in the New Age.

*"I am created new each moment."*

*"I enthusiastically receive all that life offers, deriving full benefit and learning from each experience before happily opening to the next."*

## 6 RESPONSIBILITY, LOVE

Responsibility = ability to respond, peace, truth, equilibrium and balance, service through love, strong convictions, depth of emotion, inner wisdom, harmony and beauty, home and family, idealism, enjoy helping and being responsible, balance self and others.

Service through love of all mankind. Humanitarian, responding to needs of fellowman in loving service, bringing peace and harmony.

*"I am free to respond to the true call."*

*"Divine love expressed through me opens my ability to freely respond to each moment in the way which serves the highest good for all."*

## 7 INTROSPECTION, MOVEMENT

Analysis and understanding of inner and outer worlds, growth and change, balanced quiet and activity, philosophic, spiritual awareness, conscious choice, knowing the Self, study, travel, self-control, perceptive, individual, emphasis on non-material, trust intuition, inner.

Reach spiritual perfection through knowing oneSelf and consciously creating needed movement and change through following the guidance of higher/spiritual self.

*"I seek an expanded world."*

*"I eagerly explore the expansiveness of my inner and outer worlds, opening fully to new growth through movement and change directed by my Higher Self."*

## 8 MATERIAL SATISFACTION, BALANCE

Harvest, giving and receiving, balance, justice, organization, strength, patience, manager, material rewards, practicality, business, balance material and spiritual, ambition, confidence, success, needs a strong purpose, learn material satisfaction, organized, power from mastery of physical.

Create a balance between material and spiritual world and master the material world in such a way that it totally fosters and supports spiritual freedom and expression for all in the New Age.

*"My organization brings freedom."*

*"My naturally organized mind allows me to create a fluid balance of material and spiritual expression in the world, fostering full freedom for all."*

## 9   SELFLESSNESS, HUMANITARIANISM

Completion, mastery, full spiritual consciousness developed through material experience, universal love for all, giving all of self and resources without thought of recognition or reward, reunion of all into One, spiritual wisdom, generosity, patience, compassion, philanthropy, detachment, inner transformation, strong inner conviction, idealistic, purity of expression is the key.

Transform personal love into Universal Love through giving all in the selfless service of mankind. Desire to reach perfection, achieve mastery in all expressions of Self.

*"I unconditionally give of myself."*

*"I freely give all that I am and have in the loving service of mankind, knowing that I too am perfectly loved and provided for."*

## 11   MASTER OF ILLUMINATION

Sees perfection, intuitive, high standards for self and others, energy, light, active participation, inspiration, enlightenment, leadership, spiritual channel, awareness of spiritual in relation to physical, develop and trust intuition, inspire others with purity of self.

Service to mankind through seeing and manifesting perfection and opening others to illumination and enlightenment.

*"I shine my light on the world."*

*"I am the Light in which all are illumined and in which all seeming darkness and imperfection disappear."*

## 22   MASTER BUILDER

God energy put into form, creation and manifestation of highest spiritual plans and visions, energy, power, discipline, vision, tangible manifestation, combining highest ideals with power to achieve, charismatic, must learn to focus, work for mankind.

Establish a firm foundation, based on highest spiritual truth and vision, on which to build the New World. Service to mankind through manifestation for the highest good of all.

*"I create my highest visions."*

*"I am the powerful presence for manifestation of Spiritual vision in material form."*

## 33  MASTER OF TRANSFORMATION

Compassion for all, highest love vibration, healing, teacher of teachers, inspirational, alignment of self with God and earth with Heaven, mastery of emotions, Christ consciousness, transform the world and its experiences for self and others through love of mankind.

Bring mankind to the highest state of consciousness through recognition of unconditional love for all.  Healing the planet and its inhabitants through awareness and development of unconditional love for all and through alignment with higher spiritual truth.

*"I change the world with love."*
*"I am the transformative, healing presence of unconditional love, freely and fully expressed in the world."*

## 44  MASTER OF SPIRITUAL POWER

Divine power to lead/guide mankind, organization of large projects, communities and businesses, manifesting material abundance, balancing material and spiritual world, discipline, perseverance, mastery over physical, emotional and material, authority, dominion.
Creation of universal prosperity for all mankind and organization of people and resources to physically construct the New World.

*"My power is my gift."*
*"I open the world to the abundance and prosperity surrounding us all, from which we can create anew."*

## 55  MASTER OF LIFE ENERGY

Vitality, direct higher guidance, opening new worlds and new creations, completions and new beginnings, bringing all life energy (in all forms) into harmonious and synergistic relationship, bringing the energy of new life.
Lead the way in creating the joining of all life energies to manifest new forms, new consciousness and new levels of awareness.  Bring life energy to a new level of expression.

*"All is new in me."*
*"My energy and vitality shine brightly on the world, creating more variety and aliveness in the expressions of who we are."*

## 66  MASTER OF JOYFUL ABUNDANCE

Universal love for all mankind, abundance for all through sharing and joyful expressions of love, artistic vision, sensitivity, playful innocence, seeing the Divine in all of creation, love and nurturing of all creation.
Inspire, enlighten and uplift mankind to a realization of their true nature through expression of unconditional love.

*"All is mine to give and receive."*
*"I am a joyfully expressive child, awakening the world to true abundance born of unconditional love."*

## 77  MASTER OF SPIRITUAL ENERGY

Universal wisdom and truth, sharing understanding, introducing new ways of being and seeing, master teacher, reconciling earthly and spiritual through personal experience.

Raise mass consciousness of mankind through sharing your inner awareness, personal truths and experiences and through teaching he highest spiritual wisdom which is channeled through you.

*"I am an open channel for all truth."*

*"I am an open and powerful channel for the sharing of universal wisdom and truth through my life."*

## 88  MASTER OF EVOLUTIONARY CHANGE

Understanding, wisdom, spiritual consciousness, balancing spiritual energies in worldly active expression, alignment with spiritual law, goal oriented, overcoming all fears, focus of all energy on goal.

Awaken mankind to the ability to consciously choose for change, take total responsibility for those choices and be willing to continue changing. Bring a balance of quiet and activity to allow spiritual guidance to motivate and direct all activities and choices.

*"God directs change through me."*

*"My deep inner peace empowers dramatic worldly movement aligned with the highest spiritual direction, creating fearlessness in change."*

## 99  MASTER OF UNIVERSAL LOVE

Master of love expressed as selfless service to mankind, mastery of inner and outer worlds, completion, perfection, universal truth, way-shower, leader, total detachment, unconditional forgiveness, the presence of love.

Unconditional love for all mankind manifested in leading, being and serving the highest and best to awaken all to total love for self and others.

*"I know mastery in unconditional love."*

*"I am master of my world through the expression of unconditional love and forgiveness for all of creation."*

Robert Waldon, ND, PhD

## KEEPING BALANCED ON YOUR LIFE PATH

When you are **on purpose** in travelling along your life path, you feel stable, centered and sure of your course. Each life path number will be evidenced by a different set of outer attributes or experiences. When you are **off purpose**, you are out of balance and "shaky" in your experience of yourself. During these times of imbalance, you can be assisted out of your quandary and back on course or you can lead yourself into deeper pits of despair by adopting or avoiding the characteristics of specific other numbers.

Below is a brief listing of the attributes of balanced expression for each life path number as well as the path characteristics to avoid or adopt. You should **find more detail** by referring to other sections of the book under specific path numbers.

### 1  INDEPENDENCE, CREATIVITY

Leadership, will power, initiative, independence, creativity, originality, self-confidence, conviction.

When off purpose, **avoid** characteristics of fours that will lead you to being fixed and dogmatic in what doesn't work. **Adopt** characteristics of sevens, opening to new ways of seeing and doing things.

### 2  COOPERATION, JOINING

Supportive, mediator, cooperative, adaptable, diplomatic, flexible, harmonizing, sensitive, sincere, patient.

When off purpose, **avoid** characteristics of eights that will lead you to being too concerned with keeping everyone happy. **Adopt** characteristics of fours, trusting your inner knowing and decision-making abilities.

### 3  JOYFUL SELF-EXPRESSION

Self-expressive, artistic, joyful, friendly, love of pleasure, entertaining, inspirational, imaginative, optimistic.

When off purpose, **avoid** characteristics of nines that will lead you to serving others to the exclusion of yourself. **Adopt** characteristics of sixes to create balanced and equal relationships.

## 4   DISCIPLINE, SERVICE

Responsible, leader, planner, disciplined, organized, goal-oriented, determined, conscientious, builder, courageous.

When off purpose, **avoid** characteristics of twos that will lead you to "blending in" and making things comfortable for yourself and others. **Adopt** characteristics of ones, opening to your creativity and expression of your will.

## 5   CONSTRUCTIVE FREEDOM

Curious, freedom of thought and action, perceptive, teaches new ideas, alert, discerning mind, inspirational, philosophical.

When off purpose, **avoid** characteristics of sevens that will lead you to too much thinking and analysis. **Adopt** characteristics of eights, seeking and expressing organization and balance.

## 6   RESPONSIBILITY, LOVE

Loving, appreciative, peaceful, communicative, service, love of home and family, helpful, comforting, social, gentle.

When off purpose, **avoid** characteristics of threes that will lead you to too much focus on yourself and your problems. **Adopt** characteristics of nines, focusing on others outside of yourself.

## 7   INTROSPECTION, MOVEMENT

Persistent, analytical, self-control, dreamer, individual, intuitive, explores unknown, idealistic, love of travel.

When off purpose, **avoid** characteristics of ones that will lead you to plunge ahead blindly, expressing a confused will. **Adopt** characteristics of fives, becoming thoughtful and discerning to get you back on track.

## 8   MATERIAL SATISFACTION, BALANCE

Organized, stable, balanced, success, disciplined, in control, responsible, practical, principled, unprejudiced.

When off purpose, **avoid** characteristics of fives that will lead you to be too much mental and into teaching and preaching. **Adopt** characteristics of twos, becoming adaptable, self-reliant, patient and supportive of yourself.

## 9  SELFLESSNESS, HUMANITARIANISM

Humanitarian, selfless, completion, mastery, inner wisdom, forgiving, perfectionist, peaceful, detached, leadership.

When off purpose, **avoid** characteristics of sixes that will lead you to worry about relationships and put you at the effect of how people are feeling. **Adopt** characteristics of threes, becoming more self-expressive, optimistic and inspirational.

## SOUL'S URGE

The soul's urge represents your inner motivation, your innermost, usually secret, heart's desire. This is a part of yourself which is sometimes denied or forgotten and which must be recognized and honored for you to be fully alive with joy and on purpose in your personal life. This aspect is calculated as the sum of the vowels in the full birth name expressed as a number from 1 through 9 or the Master Numbers 11 or 22.

### 1  INDEPENDENCE, CREATIVITY

Want to be a success, independent, free to act on your own, leader, pioneer, handle the "broad brush strokes" and leave details to others.

*"I am ready to begin."*
*"I confidently and creatively express my originality as I manifest my inspiration in the world."*

### 2  COOPERATION, JOINING

Want love and companionship, to be part of a team, will work hard to promote harmony.

*"I join and know love."*
*"My sensitivity to Divine guidance leads me in the reconciliation of apparent polarities and in the joining of all in shared vision and purpose."*

### 3  JOYFUL SELF-EXPRESSION

Like to express delight, active socially, express artistic talents, want home and work to reflect the beauty you enjoy creating.

"I love to express my Self."
"My full, free self-expression is an inspiration and blessing, opening the world to the experience of greater joy and happiness."

### 4  DISCIPLINE, SERVICE

Want a stable life, orderliness and systematic approach, conventional activities, disturbed by innovations or erraticism.

*"I lead from my inner strength."*
*"I easily and powerfully manifest the highest visions in material form, in loving service for the benefit and freedom of all."*

## 5   CONSTRUCTIVE FREEDOM

Want freedom, excitement, unexpected happenings, to be the one who sets the pace and direction.

*"I am created new each moment."*
*"I enthusiastically receive all that life offers, deriving full benefit and learning from each experience before happily opening to the next."*

## 6   RESPONSIBILITY, LOVE

Like to be appreciated for ability to handle responsibility, home and family focus, serve others, like beautiful surroundings.

*"I am free to respond to the true call."*
*"Divine love expressed through me opens my ability to freely respond to each moment in the way which serves the highest good for all."*

## 7   INTROSPECTION, MOVEMENT

Want time alone to develop inner resources, contemplation, dream and develop idealistic understandings, study and analyze to gain wisdom and deeper truth. From that introspection, all purposeful movement occurs.

*"I seek an expanded world."*
*"I eagerly explore the expansiveness of my inner and outer worlds, opening fully to new growth through movement and change directed by my Higher Self."*

## 8   MATERIAL SATISFACTION, BALANCE

Want to excel in the world, wealth, success, status, power, to organize, supervise or lead.

*"My organization brings freedom."*
*"My naturally organized mind allows me to create a fluid balance of material and spiritual expression in the world, fostering full freedom for all."*

## 9   SELFLESSNESS, HUMANITARIANISM

Like to help others, give to others, philanthropy, share talents and abilities.

*"I unconditionally give of myself."*
*"I freely give all that I am and have in the loving service of mankind, knowing that I too am perfectly loved and provided for."*

## 11  MASTER OF ILLUMINATION

Want to manifest spiritual views, share idealism, beauty and perfection, give of self to humanity.

*"I shine my light on the world."*
*"I am the Light in which all are illumined and in which all seeming darkness and imperfection disappear."*

## 22  MASTER BUILDER

Want to make a considerable contribution to the world, humanitarian goals, want to express power in concrete manner.

*"I create my highest visions."*
*"I am the powerful presence for manifestation of Spiritual vision in material form."*

## 33  MASTER OF TRANSFORMATION

Want to teach and inspire others, to bring the world into a state of unconditional love, to transform earth into heaven.

*"I change the world with love."*
*"I am the transformative, healing presence of unconditional love, freely and fully expressed in the world."*

## 44  MASTER OF SPIRITUAL POWER

Want to create community, manifest material mastery and abundance for all, organize people and resources of the world for greatest good of all.

*"My power is my gift."*
*"I open the world to the abundance and prosperity surrounding us all, from which we can create anew."*

## 55  MASTER OF LIFE ENERGY

Want to bring in new consciousness through joining life energies, creating synergy and harmony, open to new worlds and new creations.

*"All is new in me."*
*"My energy and vitality shine brightly on the world, creating more variety and aliveness in the expression of who we are."*

## 66   MASTER OF JOYFUL ABUNDANCE

Want to give and receive unconditional love, playful innocence, to love and nurture all of creation into abundance.

*"All is mine to give and receive."*
*"I am a joyfully expressive child, awakening the world to true abundance born of unconditional love."*

## 77   MASTER OF SPIRITUAL ENERGY

Want to share and teach your spiritual wisdom, to bring and express spiritual energy in all earthly experiences.

*"I am an open channel for all truth."*
*"I am an open and powerful channel for the sharing of universal wisdom and truth through my life."*

## 88   MASTER OF EVOLUTIONARY CHANGE

Want to change the world to operate along spiritual laws, have worldly creations totally support the spiritual, to balance worldly experience.

*"God directs change through me."*
*"My deep inner peace empowers dramatic worldly movement aligned with the highest spiritual direction, creating fearlessness in change."*

## 99   MASTER OF UNIVERSAL LOVE

Want to lead and serve the world through your unconditional love, want mastery and completion, to be the presence of love on earth.

*"I know mastery in unconditional love."*
*"I am master of my world through the expression of unconditional love and forgiveness for all of creation."*

## HOW YOU ARE SEEN

It is important to recognize how you are seen by others in order to become aware of the full impact of your presence here, the hidden expectations and the unexpressed expectations which may be effecting you and your mission. It is also of value to allow the ways in which you are perceived by others to support your own increasing self-knowledge and sense of self-worth. You can choose to use the way you are seen by others to empower you. They wouldn't see something in you which isn't there. It doesn't mean that you take every request, demand, etc. at "face value". It means you can look beneath the surface and hear what is really being called forth from you. This aspect is calculated as the sum of the consonants in the full birth name expressed as a number from 1 through 9 or one of the Master Numbers.

## 1   INDEPENDENCE, CREATIVITY

Executive, administrator, leader, promoter, original & creative approach, self-confident, self-reliant.

*"I am ready to begin."*
*"I confidently and creatively express my originality as I manifest my inspiration in the world."*

## 2   COOPERATION, JOINING

Ability to organize and handle groups, work in partnerships, facilitator, good with details, diplomatic, psychic.

*"I join and know love."*
*"My sensitivity to Divine guidance leads me in the reconciliation of apparent polarities and in the joining of all in shared vision and purpose."*

## 3   JOYFUL SELF-EXPRESSION

Enthusiastic, optimistic, talent with words, can present with imagination.

*"I love to express my Self."*
*"My full, free self-expression is an inspiration and blessing, opening the world to the experience of greater joy and happiness."*

Robert Waldon, ND, PhD

## 4 DISCIPLINE, SERVICE

Reliable, honest, organizer, manager, proceeds despite limitations, follows through, brings plans to practical form, works well with material things.

*"I lead from my inner strength."*
*"I easily and powerfully manifest the highest visions in material form, in loving service for the benefit and freedom of all."*

## 5 CONSTRUCTIVE FREEDOM

Outgoing, present-moment, good presenting ideas & working with people, clever, analytical ability, quick thinker.

*"I am created new each moment."*
*"I enthusiastically receive all that life offers, deriving full benefit and learning from each experience before happily opening to the next."*

## 6 RESPONSIBILITY, LOVE

Responsible, mediator, comforts those in need, helpful, reliable, protective.

*"I am free to respond to the true call."*
*"Divine love expressed through me opens my ability to freely respond to each moment in the way which serves the highest good for all."*

## 7 INTROSPECTION, MOVEMENT

Educator, philosopher, researcher, capable of analyzing, authority on what personal interests, unique solutions.

*"I seek an expanded world."*
*"I eagerly explore the expansiveness of my inner and outer worlds, opening fully to new growth through movement and change directed by my Higher Self."*

## 8 MATERIAL SATISFACTION, BALANCE

Powerful, influential, administrator/manager, good with money, good on large projects, realistic, practical, good judge of character.

*"My organization brings freedom."*
*"My naturally organized mind allows me to create a fluid balance of material and spiritual expression in the world, fostering full freedom for all."*

## 9   SELFLESSNESS, HUMANITARIANISM

Compassionate, understanding, wise, helpful, inspiring, counselor, teacher, philanthropist, religious/spiritual leader.

*"I unconditionally give of myself."*
*"I freely give all that I am and have in the loving service of mankind, knowing that I too am perfectly loved and provided for."*

## 11   MASTER OF ILLUMINATION

Idealistic, inspirational by example, spiritual advisor, enthusiastic, intuitive, sensitive, good at anything, teacher, good mind.

*"I shine my light on the world."*
*"I am the Light in which all are illumined and in which all seeming darkness and imperfection disappear."*

## 22   BUILDER OF NEW WORLDS

Competent, unorthodox, leading in new directions, large undertakings, capable of any work chosen, significant material accomplishments.

*"I create my highest visions."*
*"I am the powerful presence for manifestation of Spiritual vision in material form."*

## 33   MASTER OF TRANSFORMATION

Compassionate, loving, teaching others, in tune with your higher Self, spiritually aware, changing your life and the world around you for the good.

*"I change the world with love."*
*"I am the transformative, healing presence of unconditional love, freely and fully expressed in the world."*

## 44   MASTER OF SPIRITUAL POWER

Leader, organizer, manifestor of great abundance for self and others, resourceful, balancing spiritual and worldly, disciplined.

*"My power is my gift."*
*"I open the world to the abundance and prosperity surrounding us all, from which we can create anew."*

### 55   MASTER OF LIFE ENERGY

Energetic, creative, starting new things, bringing life to new forms, harmonizing expressions of life energy.

*"All is new in me."*
*"My energy and vitality shine brightly on the world, creating more variety and aliveness in the expression of who we are."*

### 66   MASTER OF JOYFUL ABUNDANCE

Loving, playfully innocent, joyfully sharing through expressions of love, inspiring, uplifting, artistic, nurturing all creation.

*"All is mine to give and receive."*
*"I am a joyfully expressive child, awakening the world to true abundance born of unconditional love."*

### 77   MASTER OF SPIRITUAL ENERGY

Wise, experienced in dealing with the world in spiritual ways, teacher, spiritual channel, super-conscious.

*"I am an open channel for all truth."*
*"I am an open and powerful channel for the sharing of universal wisdom and truth through my life."*

### 88   MASTER OF EVOLUTIONARY CHANGE

Goal oriented, fearless, focused, inspirational in the direction of change, understanding, balanced in spiritual and worldly expression.

*"God directs change through me."*
*"My deep inner peace empowers dramatic worldly movement aligned with the highest spiritual direction, creating fearlessness in change."*

### 99   MASTER OF UNIVERSAL LOVE

Loving, philanthropic, detached, forgiving, leader, serving only the highest and best, master of inner and outer world.

*"I know mastery in unconditional love."*
*"I am master of my world through the expression of unconditional love and forgiveness for all of creation."*

## OPPORTUNITIES FOR GROWTH

Your growth number represents those areas of opportunity which come to you throughout your lifetime to challenge, expand and "grow" you as a result of your choices and responses. This is not a "lesson" which comes once and is over when done correctly. This is an expanding theme of opening you ever more to the fullest experience of your true Self. This aspect is calculated as the sum of the letters in your full first name at birth expressed as a number from 1 through 9 or one of the Master Numbers. The basic learning for each number is listed below. The more consistently you respond to all that the world brings to you from the viewpoint of your growth number, the greater your expansion and growth from each opportunity.

## 1 INDEPENDENCE, CREATIVITY

Express original ideas, not give in to restrictive forces, take leadership opportunities presented you, not confuse independence with dominance.
*"I am ready to begin."*
*"I confidently and creatively express my originality as I manifest my inspiration in the world."*

## 2 COOPERATION, JOINING

Promote harmony, practice cooperation and adaptability, take care of other's needs while meeting your own, don't allow self to go totally unnoticed, express friendship and affection openly.
*"I join and know love."*
*"My sensitivity to Divine guidance leads me in the reconciliation of apparent polarities and in the joining of all in shared vision and purpose."*

## 3 JOYFUL SELF-EXPRESSION

Openly express delight and creativity, be optimistic and enthusiastic.
*"I love to express my Self."*
*"My full, free self-expression is an inspiration and blessing, opening the world to the experience of greater joy and happiness."*

## 4 DISCIPLINE, SERVICE

Not succumb to frustration, see limitations can be changed, focus on satisfaction of service not difficulty of work, be systematic & orderly to free yourself from getting lost in repetitive detail.
*"I lead from my inner strength."*
*"I easily and powerfully manifest the highest visions in material form, in loving service for the benefit and freedom of all."*

## 5   CONSTRUCTIVE FREEDOM

Must expand with versatility and adaptability, choose what works, don't be erratic or wear yourself out, don't stay too long or leave too early.
*"I am created new each moment."*
*"I enthusiastically receive all that life offers, deriving full benefit and learning from each experience before happily opening to the next."*

## 6   RESPONSIBILITY, LOVE

Learn to give and receive love and friendship, accept responsibilities, make your home a beautiful, protected, stable, helping environment.
*"I am free to respond to the true call."*
*"Divine love expressed through me opens my ability to freely respond to each moment in the way which serves the highest good for all."*

## 7   INTROSPECTION, MOVEMENT

Peace comes from within, trust intuition, learn the value of and pleasures of alone time, learn patience.
*"I seek an expanded world."*
*"I eagerly explore the expansiveness of my inner and outer worlds, opening fully to new growth through movement and change directed by my Higher Self."*

## 8   MATERIAL SATISFACTION, BALANCE

Success with balance, learn to handle money, see material as a means not and end, avoid needing more money than comfortably available, can't leave yourself out of the picture.
*"My organization brings freedom."*
*"My naturally organized mind allows me to create a fluid balance of material and spiritual expression in the world, fostering full freedom for all."*

## 9   SELFLESSNESS, HUMANITARIANISM

Give for pleasure of giving not for return or reward, allowing higher needs to take precedence over personal ambitions brings deep satisfactions.
*"I unconditionally give of myself."*
*"I freely give all that I am and have in the loving service of mankind, knowing that I too am perfectly loved and provided for."*

## 11   MASTER OF ILLUMINATION

Develop intuition, inspire others by your example, spiritual not worldly, see yourself as a Divine channel, share highest truths despite any worldly discouragements.

*"I shine my light on the world."*
*"I am the Light in which all are illumined and in which all seeming darkness and imperfection disappear."*

## 22   BUILDER OF NEW WORLDS

Learn to focus on high visions, develop a sincere desire to benefit others.

*"I create my highest visions."*
*"I am the powerful presence for manifestation of Spiritual vision in material form."*

## 33   MASTER OF TRANSFORMATION

Express unconditional love and non-judgmental transformation, develop compassion and understanding and a willingness to inspire and teach others.

*"I change the world with love."*
*"I am the transformative, healing presence of unconditional love, freely and fully expressed in the world."*

## 44   MASTER OF SPIRITUAL POWER

Go for the largest, most comprehensive vision you have, trust in your personal material abundance and abundance for all mankind, be disciplined and keep worldly activities balanced with spiritual endeavors.

*"My power is my gift."*
*"I open the world to the abundance and prosperity surrounding us all, from which we can create anew."*

## 55   MASTER OF LIFE ENERGY

Be creative, alive and energetic in pursuing your visions, be awake to completions and move on without delay, be expressive and alive with your presence.

*"All is new in me."*
*"My energy and vitality shine brightly on the world, creating more variety and aliveness in the expression of who we are."*

## 66   MASTER OF JOYFUL ABUNDANCE

Remain innocent and loving, see only the best (the love) in everything, be inspired and inspiring and abundantly expressive.

*"All is mine to give and receive."*
*"I am a joyfully expressive child, awakening the world to true abundance born of unconditional love."*

## 77   MASTER OF SPIRITUAL ENERGY

Develop and fully trust your inner awareness, recognize the value in sharing your personal truth and experiences, allow yourself to be a Spirit-filled channel for universal wisdom.

*"I am an open channel for all truth."*

*"I am an open and powerful channel for the sharing of universal wisdom and truth through my life."*

## 88   MASTER OF EVOLUTIONARY CHANGE

Stay balanced in spiritual and worldly expression, overcome all fears, focus on your goals and on higher spiritual truths, take responsibility for your choices and be willing to continue changing always.

*"God directs change through me."*

*"My deep inner peace empowers dramatic worldly movement aligned with the highest spiritual direction, creating fearlessness in change."*

## 99   MASTER OF UNIVERSAL LOVE

Serve with no expectations or attachments, learn to totally release the past through forgiveness, be willing to lead, to strive for perfection and mastery.

*"I know mastery in unconditional love."*

*"I am master of my world through the expression of unconditional love and forgiveness for all of creation."*

# LIFE BALANCING

Robert Waldon, ND, PhD

## LIFE BALANCING----—EXPRESSING YOUR WHOLENESS

We contain aspects of all symbols and all numbers within ourselves and, in order to express overall balance and mastery in life, we need to express all qualities equally well and at the appropriate times.

Below are listed the symbols and numbers along with major characteristics to help you assess their expression in your life currently.

## TAROT SYMBOLS

FOOL
**VISION** without limits or planning.
**SPONTANEITY** without fear.
*"I boldly step forward."*
*"I walk without fear into new worlds of my boundless, unlimited creation."*

MAGICIAN
**MANIFESTATION** without judgment.
**COMMUNICATION** without withhold or censorship.
*"My thought creates."*
*"The power of my thought and word magically manifest the creation of Spirit."*

HIGH PRIESTESS
**INNER TRUST** without being critical of others.
*"I trust mySelf."*
*"I am my own unlimited resource for self-knowledge, wisdom and the creation of my perfect, balanced expression."*

EMPRESS
**RECEPTIVITY** without surrender.
*"I am open to receive all good."*
*"I am nurtured by the unlimited abundance surrounding me as I equally give and receive unconditional love."*

EMPEROR
**LEADERSHIP** without control or manipulation.
*"I see and I create."*
*"I have the confidence and power to manifest my highest visions in practical form for the good of all."*

HIEROPHANT
**WISDOM** without remembering.
*"I am given the wisdom I need."*
*"I trust my higher Self to direct and empower the perfect application of my teaching and inspirational gifts."*

138

LOVERS     **LOVE** without restrictions, barriers, exclusion.
*"I love all unconditionally.*
*"Through giving total freedom and trust, I release all apparent*
*polarities and stuckness, opening to the perfect experience of*
*love in every relationship."*

CHARIOT    **CHANGE** without rigidity, resistance, stuckness.
*"I consciously choose for change."*
*"I know my chosen path and consciously focus my energies*
*affirmation of personal conviction and honoring the truth of*
*who I am in all circumstances."*

JUSTICE     **BALANCE** without prejudice or doubt.
*"I rest in balance."*
*"I trust my inner sense of justice and impartiality. With truth*
*and authenticity, I express balance and harmony in my life."*

HERMIT     MASTERY without self-cruelty (with gentleness).
*"I know truth in mastery."*
*"I experience mastery of my inner and outer worlds through*
*affirmation of personal conviction and honoring the truth of*
*who I am in all circumstances."*

WHEEL OF FORTUNE **INSPIRATION & EXPANSION** without fear.
*"All abundance is mine."*
*"I open to new opportunities and experience expansion,*
*prosperity and all abundance as I awaken to my inner*
*wholeness."*

STRENGTH/LUST  **LOVE** without judgment.
*"I love all of me."*
*"I am alive, creative, expressive and passionately in love with*
*life and all its opportunities."*

HANGED MAN   **SURRENDER & ACCEPTANCE** without
fatalism.
*"I surrender to my highest good."*
*"I surrender to the transforming Spirit within, no longer*
*content with old patterns of making myself and others limited*
*and comfortable."*

DEATH/REBIRTH     **RELEASE** without sacrifice.
*"I let go and am reborn."*
*"I confidently release all which no longer serves my highest good and open to the freedom and expansiveness of my true expression."*

ART     **CREATIVITY** without fixed opinions, restriction, worry.
*"I know unlimited creation."*
*"I creatively and confidently unite separate elements into new, unique expressions through visioning the many manifestations of wholeness."*

DEVIL     **INNOVATION** without seriousness.
*"I am open to new ways."*
*"I recognize no inner restraint as I joyfully follow my heart, opening to new opportunities and experiencing creative solutions to every apparent limitation."*

TOWER     **DISRUPTION** without defensiveness.
*"My undoing is my freedom."*
*"I experience deep inner peace in the restoration of what is highest and truest in me and in the destruction and removal of all that is false, restrictive or limiting."*

STAR     **CONFIDENCE & RADIANCE** without arrogance.
*"I clearly shine my light."*
*"My radiance, confidence and clarity of vision are shining expressions of who I am, providing light and inspiration for the world."*

MOON     **TRANSFORMATION** without deception.
*"I easily flow with my changes."*
*"I choose to support the highest truth and reality through authentic expression of who I am as I change and evolve, coming to know my wholeness."*

SUN     **VITALITY** without restriction.
*"I am the Light of the world."*
*"I am the source of inspiration, light and joy, bringing clarity and understanding to shared vision and creative exploration."*

AEON/JUDGMENT  **FORGIVENESS** without judgment or criticalness.
*"Forgiveness is my road to freedom."*
*"I bring a wealth of wisdom from personal experience to motivate and inspire the re-creation of wholeness in new forms, without evaluation or judgment."*

UNIVERSE  **WHOLENESS & COMPLETION** without exclusion.
*"I know myself in everything."*
*"I give the totality of my being and my infinite potential to the realization of transformation and the manifestation of Spirit on earth."*

## SPIRITUAL BODIES

1      **CREATIVITY** coming from the heart.
*"I am perfectly led by my heart."*
*"I totally trust and follow the guidance of my heart in all that I think, say and do."*

2      **DEVOTION** to the highest.
*"My devotion to God is all."*
*"I am devoted only to the Spirit of Love in each relationship, letting all other fears, needs and dependencies drop away."*

3      **SEEING THE POSITIVE**, see good in everything.
*"I see good and know it."*
*"I see the good in all people and events, opening me to unlimited opportunities and the experience of abundance for All."*

4      **SERVING** only the highest good for all.
*"I serve only the truest call."*
*"I set aside all fears and desires coming from myself and others and respond only to support the highest and best for all concerned."*

5      **TEACHING** by the example of how you live your life.
*"I live the lessons I would teach."*
*"I learn from every life experience, choosing only for my highest good and teaching others by my living example of truth and integrity."*

6      **CONSISTENCY**, focus and concentration.
*"My focus is my power."*
*"I experience the manifested power of my every thought and word as my natural focus creates a concentration of Spirit-filled energy."*

7      **INSPIRATION** with confidence.
*"I am inspired as I inspire."*
*"My presence alone is a blessing to all, bringing inspiration, peace and enlightenment."*

8      **PURITY** with fearlessness.
*"In my love is all healed."*
*"I am the breath of God, bringing life and wholeness to all with the purity of my loving energy."*

9     **MASTERY** with calmness.
      *"I am calm, knowing mastery of Self."*
      *"I am peaceful, gentle and calm, knowing that strength and protection are found within mastery of the Self."*


10    **FULLY VISIONARY** with courage.
      *"I hold to my true vision."*
      *"I courageously shine my light on the world, awakening and empowering living visions everywhere and giving all that I am toward their manifestation."*


11    **FULL EXPRESSION** of the highest Self.
      *"I am Divine."*
      *"I express divine perfection in my every thought, word and deed as I remember the truth of who I am."*

Robert Waldon, ND, PhD

## RELATION TO THE WORLD

1 **MANIFESTOR** "I Have"
*"I have what I choose."*
*"My strong sense of purpose and personal values powerfully create the manifestation of my desires."*

2 **SENSITIVE** "I Feel"
*"I feel the truth in my relationships."*
*"My intuition, sensitivity and understanding guide me in the perfect nurturing expression in each moment for myself and others."*

3 **WILLFUL EXPRESSER** "I Will"
*"I will and it is so."*
*"My vitality, enthusiasm and full expression create the world I choose."*

4 **HARMONIZER** "I Serve"
*"I serve the truth."*
*"My decisive, powerful action serves all in the achievement of our highest goals."*

5 **CREATOR** "I Am"
*"I am as I create."*
*"I am the perfect creation, alive in the process of becoming and actively expressing myself in my world."*

6 **COMMUNICATOR** "I Think"
*"My ideas inspire all."*
*"My powerful mind and inventive imagination expand myself and my world as they are shared."*

7 **EXPLORER** "I See"
*"I open to new vistas."*
*"I am open and free, ready to experience all the world has to offer and more."*

8 **ORGANIZER** "I Use"
*"I use all for its highest good."*
*"My practicality and sense of organization emperor excellent accomplishment in my world."*

144

9     **HUMANITARIAN** "I Analyze"
*"I analyze and see our way to Oneness."*
*"My clear vision of the whole brings all pieces of my world into harmonious and right relationship."*

11    **IDEALIST** "I Believe"
*"I believe the true and good."*
*"I hold true to my highest visions and see the perfection in all creation."*

22    **BUILDER OF NEW WORLDS** "I Know"
*"I know and all is manifest."*
*"I create my ideal world for all through the strength and clarity of my vision and the power which flows through me for its manifestation."*

33    **TRANSFORMER** "I Transform"
*"I transform my world with conscious intention."*
*"I create change through the rebirth of my personal consciousness and the transformation of my world to its highest expression."*

## NUMBERS

1    **INITIATIVE** without impulsiveness or aggressiveness.
*"I am ready to begin."*
*"I confidently and creatively express my originality as I manifest my inspiration in the world."*

2    **COOPERATION** without condescension or being protective.
*"I join and know love."*
*"My sensitivity to Divine guidance leads me in the reconciliation of apparent polarities and in the joining of all in shared vision and purpose."*

3    **SELF-EXPRESSION** without dominance.
*"I love to express mySelf."*
*"My full, free self-expression is an inspiration and blessing, opening the world to the experience of greater joy and happiness."*

4    **AUTHORITY** without dogmatism or inflexibility.
*"I lead from my inner strength."*
*"I easily and powerfully manifest the highest visions in material form, in loving service for the benefit and freedom of all."*

5    **CREATIVITY** without restlessness or discontent.
*"I am created new each moment."*
*"I enthusiastically receive all that life offers, deriving full benefit and learning from each experience before happily opening to the next."*

6    **RESPONSIBILITY** without martyrdom.
*"I am free to respond to the true call."*
*"Divine love expressed through me opens my ability to freely respond to each moment in the way which serves the highest good for all."*

7    **EXPLORATION** without obsession or fixation.
*"I seek an expanded world."*
*"I eagerly explore the expansiveness of my inner and outer worlds, opening fully to new growth through movement and change directed by my Higher Self."*

8    **ORGANIZATION** without rigidity.
*"My organization brings freedom."*
*"My naturally organized mind allows me to create a fluid balance of material and spiritual expression in the world, fostering full freedom for all."*

9    **SELFLESSNESS** without sacrifice.
*"I unconditionally give of myself."*
*"I freely give all that I am and have in the loving service of mankind, knowing that I too am perfectly loved and provided for."*

11   **ILLUMINATION** with active participation.
*"I shine my light on the world."*
*"I am the Light in which all are illumined and in which all seeming darkness and imperfection disappear."*

22   **MANIFESTATION** with vision and power.
*"I create my highest visions."*
*"I am the powerful presence for manifestation of Spiritual vision in material form."*

33   **TRANSFORMATION** with compassion.
*"I change the world with love."*
*"I am the transformative, healing presence of unconditional love, freely and fully expressed in the world."*

44   **POWER** with balance.
*"My power is my gift."*
*"I open the world to the abundance and prosperity surrounding us all, from which we can create anew."*

55   **NEW BEGINNINGS** with synergy and vitality.
*"All is new in me."*
*"My energy and vitality shine brightly on the world, creating more variety and aliveness in the expressions of who we are."*

66   **ABUNDANCE** with unconditional sharing.
*"All is mine to give and receive."*
*"I am a joyfully expressive child, awakening the world to true abundance born of unconditional love."*

77   **UNIVERSAL WISDOM** with experience and understanding.

*"I am an open channel for all truth."*
*"I am an open and powerful channel for the sharing of universal wisdom and truth through my life."*

88     **EVOLUTION AND CHANGE** with consciousness.
    *"God directs change through me."*
    *"My deep inner peace empowers dramatic worldly movement aligned with the highest spiritual direction, creating fearlessness in change."*

99     **UNCONDITIONAL LOVE** with detachment.
    *"I know mastery in unconditional love."*
    *"I am master of my world through the expression of unconditional love and forgiveness for all of creation."*

# ADDITIONAL
# WORKSHEETS

Robert Waldon, ND, PhD

## PERSONAL INDEX

(You will fill this chart in from the Chapter on Calculations.)

| LINE | | Number/ Symbol | Personal Page | Book # |
|---|---|---|---|---|
| 1 | Lifetime Symbol | _____ | _____ | ----43 |
| 2 | Spiritual Symbol | _____ | _____ | ----43 |
| 3 | Personal Cycle | _____ | _____ | ----59 |
| 4 | Universal Year | _____ | _____ | ----73 |
| 5 | Personal Year | _____ | _____ | ----73 |
| | | | | |
| 6 | Outer Harmony | _____ | _____ | ----82 |
| 7 | Inner Peace | _____ | _____ | ----84 |
| 8 | Past Accomplishments | _____ | _____ | ----86 |
| 9 | Spiritual Path | _____ | _____ | ----98 |
| 10 | God's Gift | _____ | _____ | ----90 |
| | | | | |
| 11 | Physical | _____ | _____ | ---101 |
| 12 | Emotional | _____ | _____ | ---103 |
| 13 | Mental | _____ | _____ | ---105 |
| 14 | Spiritual Creativity | _____ | _____ | ---108 |
| | | | | |
| 15 | Collective Experience | _____ | _____ | ---116 |
| 16 | Life Path | _____ | _____ | ---116 |
| 17 | Ultimate Lifetime Goal | _____ | _____ | ---116 |
| 18 | Balance on Life Path | _____ | _____ | ---123 |
| 19 | Soul's Urge | _____ | _____ | ---126 |
| 20 | How You Are Seen | _____ | _____ | ---130 |
| 21 | Growth | _____ | _____ | ---134 |
| | | | | |
| 22 | Balancing Expression | _____ | _____ | ---139 |

# PERSONAL INDEX

(You will fill this chart in from the Chapter on Calculations.)

| LINE | | Number/ Symbol | Personal Page | Book # |
|---|---|---|---|---|
| 1 | Lifetime Symbol | _____ | _____ | ----43 |
| 2 | Spiritual Symbol | _____ | _____ | ----43 |
| 3 | Personal Cycle | _____ | _____ | ----59 |
| 4 | Universal Year | _____ | _____ | ----73 |
| 5 | Personal Year | _____ | _____ | ----73 |
| 6 | Outer Harmony | _____ | _____ | ----82 |
| 7 | Inner Peace | _____ | _____ | ----84 |
| 8 | Past Accomplishments | _____ | _____ | ----86 |
| 9 | Spiritual Path | _____ | _____ | ----98 |
| 10 | God's Gift | _____ | _____ | ----90 |
| 11 | Physical | _____ | _____ | ---101 |
| 12 | Emotional | _____ | _____ | ---103 |
| 13 | Mental | _____ | _____ | ---105 |
| 14 | Spiritual Creativity | _____ | _____ | ---108 |
| 15 | Collective Experience | _____ | _____ | ---116 |
| 16 | Life Path | _____ | _____ | ---116 |
| 17 | Ultimate Lifetime Goal | _____ | _____ | ---116 |
| 18 | Balance on Life Path | _____ | _____ | ---123 |
| 19 | Soul's Urge | _____ | _____ | ---126 |
| 20 | How You Are Seen | _____ | _____ | ---130 |
| 21 | Growth | _____ | _____ | ---134 |
| 22 | Balancing Expression | _____ | _____ | ---139 |

**Robert Waldon, ND, PhD**

## PERSONAL INDEX

(You will fill this chart in from the Chapter on Calculations.)

| LINE | | Number/ Symbol | Personal Page | Book # |
|---|---|---|---|---|
| 1 | Lifetime Symbol | _____ | _____ | ----43 |
| 2 | Spiritual Symbol | _____ | _____ | ----43 |
| 3 | Personal Cycle | _____ | _____ | ----59 |
| 4 | Universal Year | _____ | _____ | ----73 |
| 5 | Personal Year | _____ | _____ | ----73 |
| 6 | Outer Harmony | _____ | _____ | ----82 |
| 7 | Inner Peace | _____ | _____ | ----84 |
| 8 | Past Accomplishments | _____ | _____ | ----86 |
| 9 | Spiritual Path | _____ | _____ | ----98 |
| 10 | God's Gift | _____ | _____ | ----90 |
| 11 | Physical | _____ | _____ | ---101 |
| 12 | Emotional | _____ | _____ | ---103 |
| 13 | Mental | _____ | _____ | ---105 |
| 14 | Spiritual Creativity | _____ | _____ | ---108 |
| 15 | Collective Experience | _____ | _____ | ---116 |
| 16 | Life Path | _____ | _____ | ---116 |
| 17 | Ultimate Lifetime Goal | _____ | _____ | ---116 |
| 18 | Balance on Life Path | _____ | _____ | ---123 |
| 19 | Soul's Urge | _____ | _____ | ---126 |
| 20 | How You Are Seen | _____ | _____ | ---130 |
| 21 | Growth | _____ | _____ | ---134 |
| 22 | Balancing Expression | _____ | _____ | ---139 |

# PERSONAL INDEX

(You will fill this chart in from the Chapter on Calculations.)

| LINE | | Number/<br>Symbol | Personal<br>Page | Book<br># |
|------|--------------------------|----------|----------|-------|
| 1 | Lifetime Symbol | _____ | _____ | ----43 |
| 2 | Spiritual Symbol | _____ | _____ | ----43 |
| 3 | Personal Cycle | _____ | _____ | ----59 |
| 4 | Universal Year | _____ | _____ | ----73 |
| 5 | Personal Year | _____ | _____ | ----73 |
| | | | | |
| 6 | Outer Harmony | _____ | _____ | ----82 |
| 7 | Inner Peace | _____ | _____ | ----84 |
| 8 | Past Accomplishments | _____ | _____ | ----86 |
| 9 | Spiritual Path | _____ | _____ | ----98 |
| 10 | God's Gift | _____ | _____ | ----90 |
| | | | | |
| 11 | Physical | _____ | _____ | ---101 |
| 12 | Emotional | _____ | _____ | ---103 |
| 13 | Mental | _____ | _____ | ---105 |
| 14 | Spiritual Creativity | _____ | _____ | ---108 |
| | | | | |
| 15 | Collective Experience | _____ | _____ | ---116 |
| 16 | Life Path | _____ | _____ | ---116 |
| 17 | Ultimate Lifetime Goal | _____ | _____ | ---116 |
| 18 | Balance on Life Path | _____ | _____ | ---123 |
| 19 | Soul's Urge | _____ | _____ | ---126 |
| 20 | How You Are Seen | _____ | _____ | ---130 |
| 21 | Growth | _____ | _____ | ---134 |
| | | | | |
| 22 | Balancing Expression | _____ | _____ | ---139 |

## SPIRITUAL BODIES

1   Soul - creativity, humility
2   Negative Mind - longing to belong, devotion
3   Positive Mind - equality
4   Neutral Mind - service
5   Physical Body - teacher by example
6   Third Eye - one pointed concentration
7   Aura - mercy, uplifting
8   Prana - purity, healing
9   Subtle Body - calmness, mastery
10  Radiant Body - visionary, royal courage
11  Entirety, Perfection of Being - the infinite

## CURRENT SOUL CONNECTIONS

| Name | Outer Harmony | Inner Peace | Past Accomp. | Spiritual Path | God's Gift |
|------|---------------|-------------|--------------|----------------|------------|
|      |               |             |              |                |            |

## SPIRITUAL CHALLENGES

| Name | Outer Harmony | Inner Peace | Past Accomp. | Spiritual Path | God's Gift |
|------|---------------|-------------|--------------|----------------|------------|
|      |               |             |              |                |            |

## SPIRITUAL BODIES

1  Soul - creativity, humility
2  Negative Mind - longing to belong, devotion
3  Positive Mind - equality
4  Neutral Mind - service
5  Physical Body - teacher by example
6  Third Eye - one pointed concentration
7  Aura - mercy, uplifting
8  Prana - purity, healing
9  Subtle Body - calmness, mastery
10  Radiant Body - visionary, royal courage
11  Entirety, Perfection of Being - the infinite

## CURRENT SOUL CONNECTIONS

| Name | Outer Harmony | Inner Peace | Past Accomp. | Spiritual Path | God's Gift |
|------|---------------|-------------|--------------|----------------|------------|
|      |               |             |              |                |            |

## SPIRITUAL CHALLENGES

| Name | Outer Harmony | Inner Peace | Past Accomp. | Spiritual Path | God's Gift |
|------|---------------|-------------|--------------|----------------|------------|
|      |               |             |              |                |            |

Robert Waldon, ND, PhD

## RELATIONSHIP TO THE WORLD

1   Manifestor - "I Have"
2   Sensitive - "I Feel"
3   Willful Expresser - "I Will"
4   Harmonizer - "I Serve"
5   Creator - "I Am"
6   Communicator - "I Think"
7   Explorer - "I See"
8   Organizer - "I Use"
9   Humanitarian - "I Analyze"
11  Idealist - "I Believe"
22  Builder of New Worlds - "I Know"
33  Transformer - "I Desire"

## PAST SOUL CONNECTIONS

| Name (inspirational) | Physical Creative (blood tie) | Emotional (love bond) | Mental (cognate) |
|---|---|---|---|

## WORLDLY CHALLENGES

| Name | Physical Creative | Emotional | Mental |
|---|---|---|---|

156

## RELATIONSHIP TO THE WORLD

1   Manifestor - "I Have"
2   Sensitive - "I Feel"
3   Willful Expresser - "I Will"
4   Harmonizer - "I Serve"
5   Creator - "I Am"
6   Communicator - "I Think"
7   Explorer - "I See"
8   Organizer - "I Use"
9   Humanitarian - "I Analyze"
11   Idealist - "I Believe"
22   Builder of New Worlds - "I Know"
33   Transformer - "I Desire"

## PAST SOUL CONNECTIONS

| | Physical Creative | Emotional | Mental |
|---|---|---|---|
| Name (inspirational) | (blood tie) | (love bond) | (cognate) |

## WORLDLY CHALLENGES

| Name | Physical Creative | Emotional | Mental |
|---|---|---|---|

Robert Waldon, ND, PhD

# Robert Waldon, ND, PhD

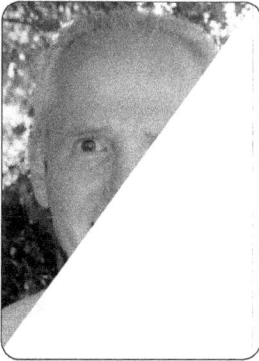

**Natural Health Consultant**

**Specialized Kinesiologist**

**Ayurvedic Lifestyle Consultant**

**Touch For Health Instructor**

**Energetic Life Balancing Instructor**

**Reiki Master Teacher**

**B.A. in Psychology**

**Ph.D. in Holistic Health**

**ND in Natural Healing**

Robert has doctorates in Naturopathy and Holistic Health as well as postgraduate degrees in Psychology, Education, Business and Finance and is a Certified Financial Planner. His well-rounded educational background and experience enrich his versatile style of presentation to educate and entertain, to inform and inspire. Robert's unique talent invites individuals to select effective tools and explore optimum possibilities leading to personal and professional fulfillment.

Robert spent the first four years of his career as an elementary school teacher. For the next ten years, he owned a successful Financial Planning firm designing Selective Executive Compensation and Benefit Plans for both private and Fortune 500 corporations. Since then, as founder and CEO of the Energetic Life Balancing Institute, Robert has trained and certified hundreds of professional practitioners across the U.S. and presented keynote programs for national business, health and educational conferences. He is a published author and has produced educational, motivational and training videos.

Robert designs and presents workshops and seminars nationwide, educating, inspiring and motivating individuals from a variety of professions and businesses. He empowers participants to achieve personal peak performance and increased levels of personal wellness and professional effectiveness.

**Reunion Ministries**
17664 Greenridge Road
Hidden Valley Lake, CA 95467

**(800) 919-2392**
**Robert@ReunionMinistries.org**

www.ingramcontent.com/pod-product-compliance
Lightning Source LLC
Chambersburg PA
CBHW061724020426
42331CB00006B/1083